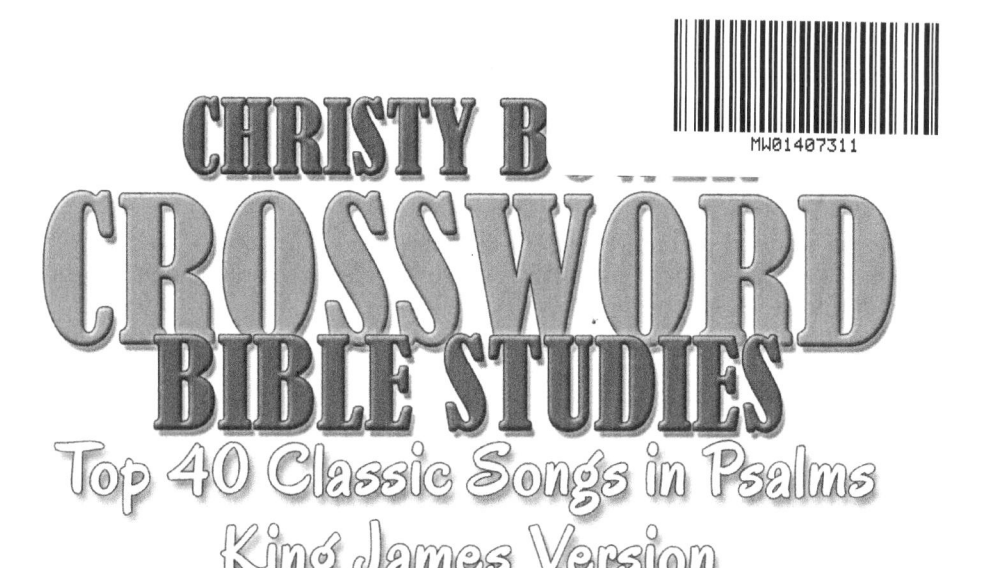

CHRISTY BOWER
CROSSWORD BIBLE STUDIES
Top 40 Classic Songs in Psalms
King James Version

All Clues are taken directly from the 1611 edition of the King James Version (KJV).
Crossword Bible Studies: Top 40 Classic Songs in Psalms (KJV) © 2017 Christy Bower
These puzzles are reproducible if you purchased the book.
www.CrosswordBibleStudies.com

Thank You

Thank you for purchasing this volume of Crossword Bible Studies. You just put a meal on my table. Your support enables me to continue to produce other resources to help people grow in their faith.

How to Use This Book

Each puzzle in this volume is based on one chapter of the Bible. The clues come directly from the 1611 edition of the King James Version (KJV). At the end of each clue is a verse reference so you can look up the verse, fill in the blank, and complete your puzzle. Guaranteed success!

Reproducible Puzzles

If you purchased this book, the author grants you the right to reproduce the puzzles for your family, church, or school. Please do not remove or alter the copyright information, instructions, and web address at the bottom of each page. You may not distribute digital copies and you may not resell either printed or digital copies.

About Christy Bower

Christy Bower, author of Crossword Bible Studies (12 Volumes on the New Testament), continues to make learning the Bible fun by responding to reader requests for crosswords on the Old Testament. Christy has a Master of Biblical Studies at Multnomah Biblical Seminary and she's the author of more than two dozen books. American Christian Writers has twice named Christy "Writer of the Year" and two of her books with Discovery House (Our Daily Bread Ministries) have gone into four or more printings.

Crossword Bible Studies – Top 40 Classic Songs in Psalms: King James Version

Copyright © 2017 Christy Bower

http://christybower.com/email/

ISBN-13: 978-1974142583

ISBN-10: 1974142582

Cover image is in the public domain.

The 1611 edition of the King James Version (KJV) is in the public domain.

All Clues are taken directly from the 1611 edition of the King James Version (KJV).
Crossword Bible Studies: Top 40 Classic Songs in Psalms (KJV) © 2017 Christy Bower
These puzzles are reproducible if you purchased the book.
www.CrosswordBibleStudies.com

Top 40 Classic Songs in Psalms

Did you know psalms were written as songs? We think of them as poetry, but they were really lyrics. Some psalms were songs of praise to God and others were brokenhearted laments begging for God's aid to ease sorrow and suffering. Many of the psalms were petitions asking for God's help in desperate situations. Others were reflecting on God's word or God's achievements in the past as a source of encouragement and hope.

While many psalms were for personal use, others were composed for corporate worship, often in a call-and-response pattern. The term "Selah" appears often and, although the meaning is unclear, it appears to be a pause or musical interlude in the song for the worshippers to reflect on the meaning.

Some songs were for specific purposes, such as a royal wedding, or specific feasts and festivals on the Hebrew calendar. The Psalms of Ascent are a group of songs sung while making the pilgrimage to the Temple in Jerusalem.

Today, we think of Psalms as one book, but it originally consisted of five books. Many believe these divisions reflect changes in the content of the songs that coincides with the themes found in the Torah or Pentateuch (the first five books of the Bible). Or it could be that these groups of Psalms had a more practical explanation, such as that's simply where one scroll ended and another began.

Remarkably, these songs have stood the test of time. People still find comfort and hope in the pages of the Psalms. With or without music, the lyrics still resonate in our hearts as we each search for God's ever-present help in times of trouble. From the mountains and valleys of life, we hear our own struggles voiced in different Psalms. A lot has changed in several thousand years, but not the cry of the heart. And not the God who hears us.

These forty Psalms have remained familiar sources of blessing from generation to generation, making them the "Top 40" Classic Songs in Psalms.

Top 40 List

Psalm 1	Psalm 34	Psalm 67	Psalm 115
Psalm 8	Psalm 37	Psalm 73	Psalm 118
Psalm 16	Psalm 40	Psalm 84	Psalm 119
Psalm 18	Psalm 42	Psalm 91	Psalm 121
Psalm 19	Psalm 46	Psalm 95	Psalm 122
Psalm 23	Psalm 50	Psalm 96	Psalm 136
Psalm 24	Psalm 51	Psalm 100	Psalm 137
Psalm 27	Psalm 56	Psalm 103	Psalm 138
Psalm 32	Psalm 62	Psalm 107	Psalm 139
Psalm 33	Psalm 63	Psalm 112	Psalm 145

To make sure you don't miss future releases, join Christy's Friend List (one or two emails per month):

http://christybower.com/email/

All Clues are taken directly from the 1611 edition of the King James Version (KJV).
Crossword Bible Studies: Top 40 Classic Songs in Psalms (KJV) © 2017 Christy Bower
These puzzles are reproducible if you purchased the book.
www.CrosswordBibleStudies.com

Also Available in the Crossword Bible Studies (Themes) Series

All Clues are taken directly from the 1611 edition of the King James Version (KJV).
Crossword Bible Studies: Top 40 Classic Songs in Psalms (KJV) © 2017 Christy Bower
These puzzles are reproducible if you purchased the book.
www.CrosswordBibleStudies.com

Crossword Bible Studies (12 Volumes on the New Testament)

This series features one puzzle for each chapter of the New Testament: 260 puzzles!!

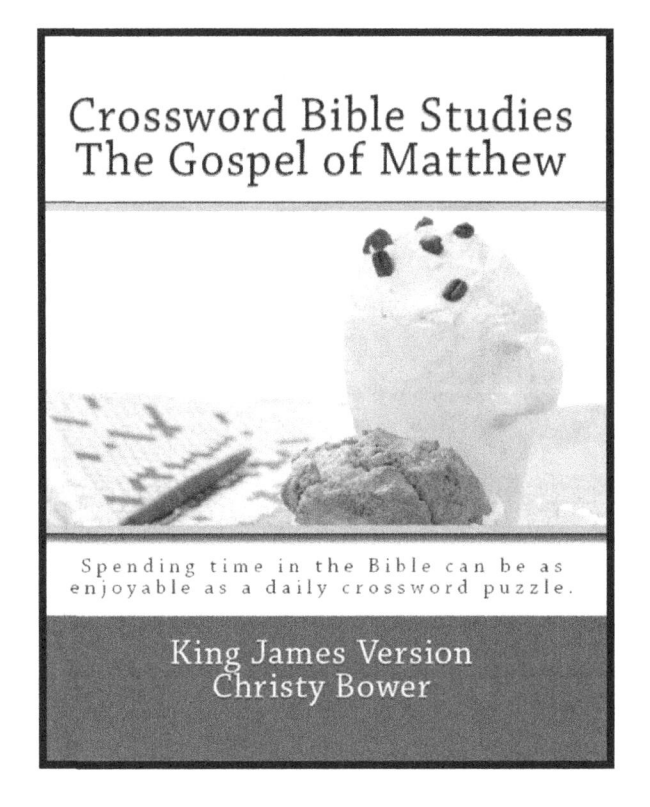

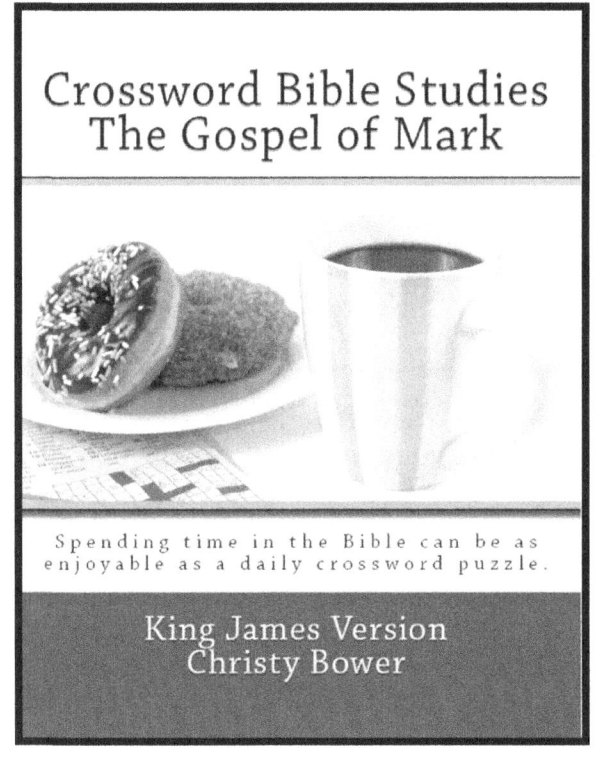

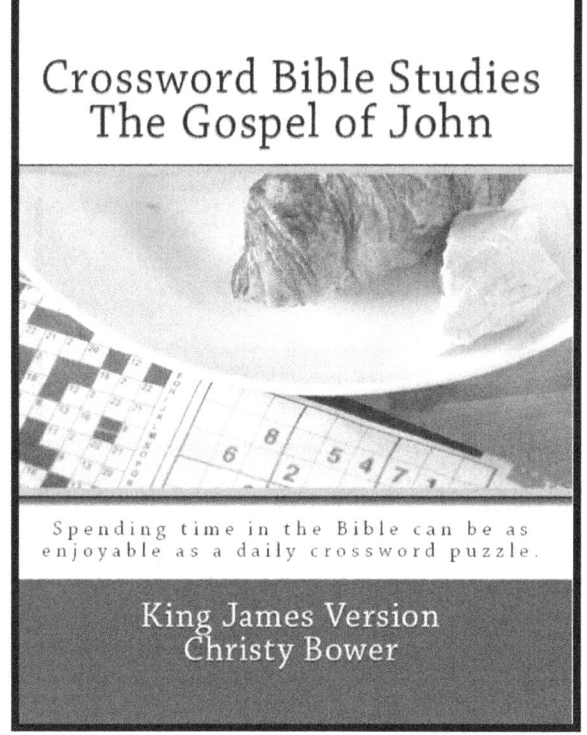

Crossword Bible Studies
The Gospel of Matthew

Spending time in the Bible can be as enjoyable as a daily crossword puzzle.

King James Version
Christy Bower

Crossword Bible Studies
The Gospel of Luke

Spending time in the Bible can be as enjoyable as a daily crossword puzzle.

King James Version
Christy Bower

Crossword Bible Studies
The Gospel of Mark

Spending time in the Bible can be as enjoyable as a daily crossword puzzle.

King James Version
Christy Bower

Crossword Bible Studies
The Gospel of John

Spending time in the Bible can be as enjoyable as a daily crossword puzzle.

King James Version
Christy Bower

All Clues are taken directly from the 1611 edition of the King James Version (KJV).
Crossword Bible Studies: Top 40 Classic Songs in Psalms (KJV) © 2017 Christy Bower
These puzzles are reproducible if you purchased the book.
www.CrosswordBibleStudies.com

Crossword Bible Studies
The Acts of the Apostles

Spending time in the Bible can be as enjoyable as a daily crossword puzzle.

King James Version
Christy Bower

Crossword Bible Studies
First & Second Corinthians

Spending time in the Bible can be as enjoyable as a daily crossword puzzle.

King James Version
Christy Bower

Crossword Bible Studies
Romans

Spending time in the Bible can be as enjoyable as a daily crossword puzzle.

King James Version
Christy Bower

Crossword Bible Studies
Galatians to Colossians

Spending time in the Bible can be as enjoyable as a daily crossword puzzle.

King James Version
Christy Bower

All Clues are taken directly from the 1611 edition of the King James Version (KJV).
Crossword Bible Studies: Top 40 Classic Songs in Psalms (KJV) © 2017 Christy Bower
These puzzles are reproducible if you purchased the book.
www.CrosswordBibleStudies.com

Crossword Bible Studies
First Thessalonians to Philemon

Spending time in the Bible can be as enjoyable as a daily crossword puzzle.

King James Version
Christy Bower

Crossword Bible Studies
First Peter to Jude

Spending time in the Bible can be as enjoyable as a daily crossword puzzle.

King James Version
Christy Bower

Crossword Bible Studies
Hebrews & James

Spending time in the Bible can be as enjoyable as a daily crossword puzzle.

King James Version
Christy Bower

Crossword Bible Studies
Revelation

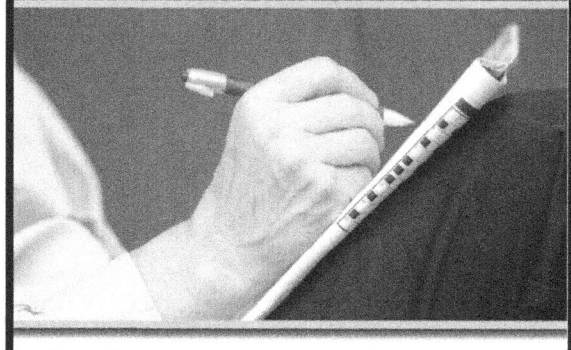

Spending time in the Bible can be as enjoyable as a daily crossword puzzle.

King James Version
Christy Bower

All Clues are taken directly from the 1611 edition of the King James Version (KJV).
Crossword Bible Studies: Top 40 Classic Songs in Psalms (KJV) © 2017 Christy Bower
These puzzles are reproducible if you purchased the book.
www.CrosswordBibleStudies.com

Psalm 1

Across

2. in his law doth he _____ (1:2)
3. his leaf also shall not _____ (1:3)
4. The ungodly are not so: but are like the _____ (1:4)
5. bringeth forth his fruit in his _____ (1:3)
8. whatsoever he doeth shall _____ (1:3)
10. walketh not in the _____ of the ungodly (1:1)
11. For the LORD knoweth the _____ of the righteous (1:6)
14. which the _____ driveth away (1:4)
15. the _____ of the LORD (1:2)
16. meditate day and _____ (1:2)
19. But his _____ is in the law of the LORD (1:2)
20. the law of the _____ (1:2)
21. And he shall be like a _____ (1:3)
22. nor standeth in the way of _____ (1:1)
23. Therefore the ungodly shall not _____ (1:5)

Down

1. the way of the _____ (1:6)
4. nor sinners in the _____ of the righteous (1:5)
6. shall not stand in the _____ (1:5)
7. that bringeth forth his _____ in his season (1:3)
8. like a tree _____ by the rivers of water (1:3)
9. nor sitteth in the _____ of the scornful (1:1)
12. The _____ are not so (1:4)
13. a tree planted by the rivers of _____ (1:3)
17. the way of the ungodly shall _____ (1:6)
18. _____ is the man that walketh not in the counsel of the ungodly (1:1)

All Clues are taken directly from the 1611 edition of the King James Version (KJV).
Crossword Bible Studies: Top 40 Classic Songs in Psalms (KJV) © 2017 Christy Bower
These puzzles are reproducible if you purchased the book.
www.CrosswordBibleStudies.com

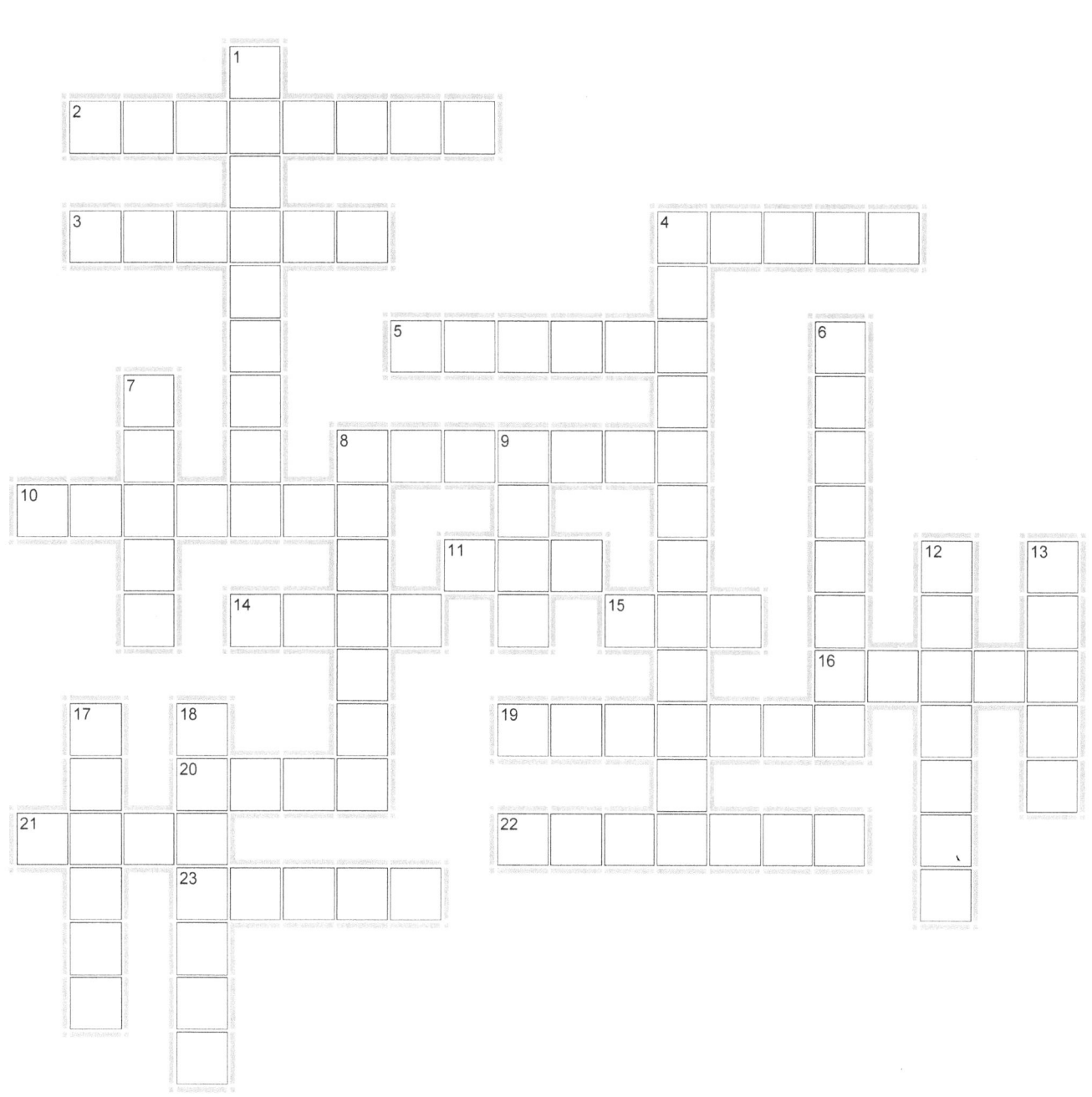

Psalm 1

Psalm 8

Across

1. For thou hast made him a little lower than the _____ (8:5)
4. O LORD our Lord, how _____ is thy name (8:9)
6. Lord, how excellent is thy _____ in all the earth! (8:1)
8. how excellent is thy name in all the _____! (8:9)
11. O _____ our Lord (8:1)
12. the moon and the _____ (8:3)
13. that thou mightest still the _____ (8:2)
16. When I _____ thy heavens (8:3)
18. dominion over the works of thy _____ (8:6)
20. the _____ of the sea (8:8)
21. The fowl of the _____ (8:8)
22. All _____ and oxen, yea, and the beasts (8:7)
23. the stars, which thou hast _____ (8:3)

Down

1. still the enemy and the _____ (8:2)
2. hast _____ him with glory and honour (8:5)
3. hast thou ordained _____ because of thine enemies (8:2)
5. whatsoever passeth through the paths of the _____ (8:8)
7. What is man, that thou art _____ of him? (8:4)
9. set thy glory above the _____ (8:1)
10. who hast set thy _____ (8:1)
14. thy heavens, the work of thy _____ (8:3)
15. Out of the _____ of babes and sucklings (8:2)
17. Thou madest him to have _____ over the works of thy hands (8:6)
19. the beasts of the _____ (8:7)
20. thou hast put all things under his _____ (8:6)

All Clues are taken directly from the 1611 edition of the King James Version (KJV).
Crossword Bible Studies: Top 40 Classic Songs in Psalms (KJV) © 2017 Christy Bower
These puzzles are reproducible if you purchased the book.
www.CrosswordBibleStudies.com

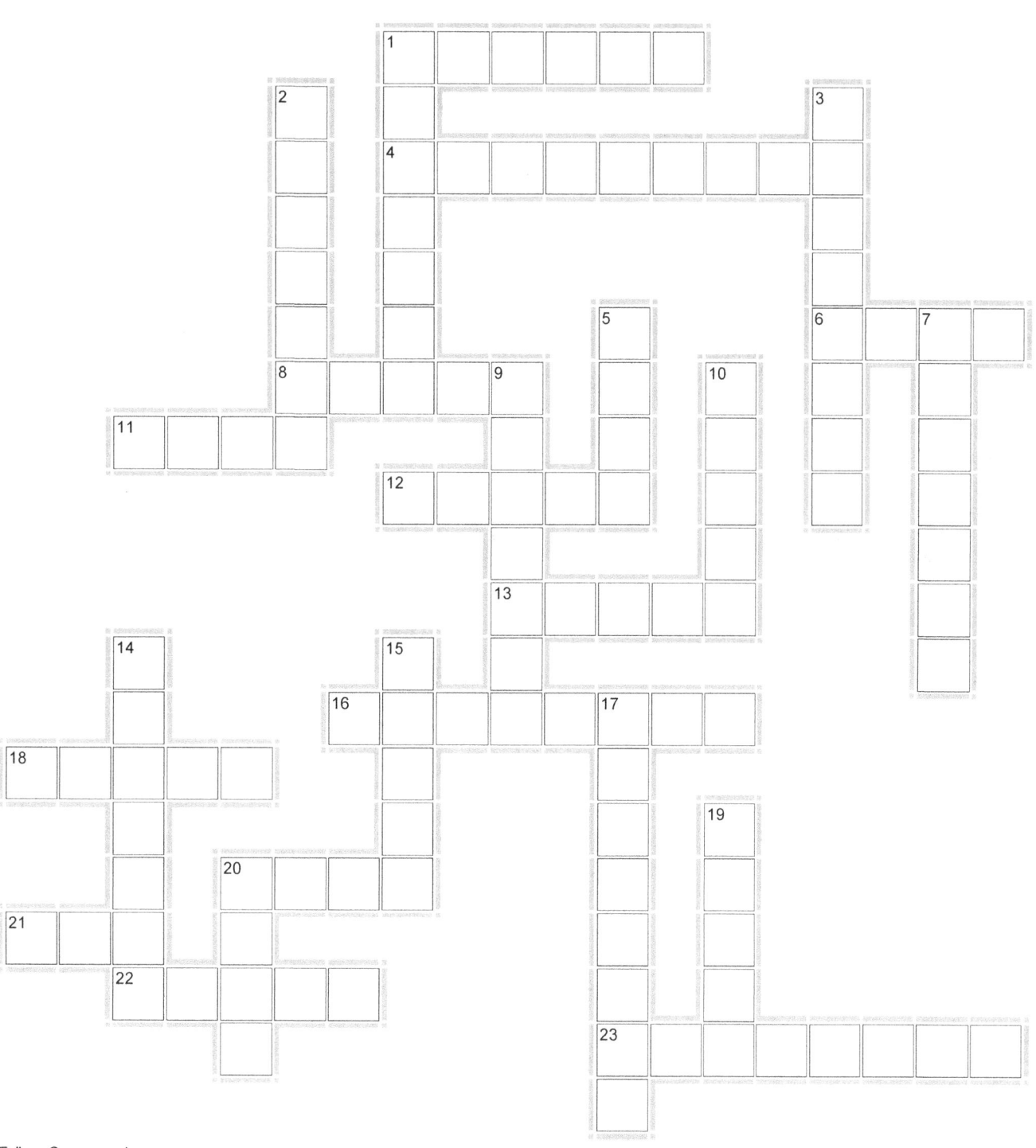

Psalm 8

Psalm 16

Across

3. in thy _____ is fulness of joy (16:11)
4. I will _____ the Lord (16:7)
7. in thee do I put my _____ (16:1)
9. thou hast said unto the Lord, Thou art my _____ (16:2)
10. the saints that are in the _____ (16:3)
12. wilt thou suffer thine Holy One to see _____ (16:10)
14. I shall not be _____ (16:8)
16. O my _____, thou hast said unto the Lord (16:2)
17. to the excellent, in whom is all my _____ (16:3)
20. For thou wilt not leave my soul in _____ (16:10)
21. _____ me, O God (16:1)
22. he is at my _____ hand (16:8)
23. nor take up their _____ into my lips (16:4)
24. The lines are fallen unto me in _____ places (16:6)
25. Therefore my _____ is glad (16:9)
26. the Lord, who hath given me _____ (16:7)

Down

1. I have a goodly _____ (16:6)
2. and my _____ rejoiceth (16:9)
3. Thou wilt shew me the _____ of life (16:11)
5. neither wilt thou _____ thine Holy One to see corruption (16:10)
6. but to the _____ that are in the earth (16:3)
8. Their _____ shall be multiplied that hasten after another god (16:4)
11. my flesh also shall rest in _____ (16:9)
13. instruct me in the _____ seasons (16:7)
15. their drink _____ of blood will I not offer (16:4)
18. The Lord is the portion of mine _____ and of my cup (16:5)
19. at thy right hand there are _____ for evermore (16:11)

All Clues are taken directly from the 1611 edition of the King James Version (KJV).
Crossword Bible Studies: Top 40 Classic Songs in Psalms (KJV) © 2017 Christy Bower
These puzzles are reproducible if you purchased the book.
www.CrosswordBibleStudies.com

Psalm 16

Psalm 18

Across

1. For thou hast girded me with strength unto the _____: thou hast subdued under me those that rose up against me (18:39)
5. For thou wilt save the _____ people; but wilt bring down high looks (18:27)
7. the floods of ungodly men made me _____ (18:4)
11. For all his judgments were before me, and I did not put away his _____ from me (18:22)
13. He maketh my feet like hinds' feet, and setteth me upon my high _____ (18:33)
14. He bowed the heavens also, and came down: and darkness was under his _____ (18:9)
17. He teacheth my hands to war, so that a bow of _____ is broken by mine arms (18:34)
18. Thou hast also given me the _____ of thy salvation (18:35)
21. he rode upon a _____, and did fly: yea, he did fly upon the wings of the wind (18:10)
22. thou liftest me up above those that rise up against me: thou hast delivered me from the _____ man (18:48)
23. He delivered me from my _____ enemy, and from them which hated me: for they were too strong for me (18:17)
25. I was also upright before him, and I kept myself from mine _____ (18:23)
28. He sent from above, he took me, he drew me out of many _____ (18:16)
29. Thou hast _____ me from the strivings of the people (18:43)
31. For by thee I have run through a troop; and by my God have I leaped over a _____ (18:29)
33. They prevented me in the day of my calamity: but the _____ was my stay (18:18)
34. Yea, he sent out his _____, and scattered them; and he shot out lightnings (18:14)
35. He brought me forth also into a large place; he delivered me, because he _____ in me (18:19)
36. For I have kept the ways of the LORD, and have not wickedly _____ from my God (18:21)

Down

2. Therefore will I give _____ unto thee, O LORD, among the heathen, and sing praises unto thy name (18:49)
3. It is God that avengeth me, and subdueth the _____ under me (18:47)
4. In my _____ I called upon the LORD, and cried unto my God: he heard my voice (18:6)
6. The LORD is my rock, and my _____, and my deliverer; my God, my strength, in whom I will trust; my buckler, and the horn of my salvation, and my high tower (18:2)
8. They cried, but there was none to save them: even unto the LORD, but he _____ them not (18:41)
9. the snares of _____ prevented me (18:5)
10. the foundations of the world were discovered at thy rebuke, O LORD, at the blast of the breath of thy _____ (18:15)
12. Then the earth _____ and trembled; the foundations also of the hills moved (18:7)
15. The LORD liveth; and blessed be my rock; and let the God of my _____ be exalted (18:46)
16. At the brightness that was before him his thick clouds passed, hail stones and coals of _____ (18:12)
19. He made darkness his _____ place; his pavilion round about him were dark waters and thick clouds of the skies (18:11)
20. With the _____ thou wilt shew thyself pure (18:26)
23. There went up a _____ out of his nostrils, and fire out of his mouth devoured: coals were kindled by it (18:8)
24. With the _____ thou wilt shew thyself merciful (18:25)
26. The LORD also _____ in the heavens, and the Highest gave his voice; hail stones and coals of fire (18:13)
27. I will _____ thee, O LORD, my strength (18:1)
28. As for God, his way is perfect: the _____ of the LORD is tried (18:30)
29. Great deliverance giveth he to his king; and sheweth mercy to his anointed, to _____, and to his seed for evermore (18:50)
30. For thou wilt light my _____: the LORD my God will enlighten my darkness (18:28)
32. I will _____ upon the LORD, who is worthy to be praised: so shall I be saved from mine enemies (18:3)

All Clues are taken directly from the 1611 edition of the King James Version (KJV).
Crossword Bible Studies: Top 40 Classic Songs in Psalms (KJV) © 2017 Christy Bower
These puzzles are reproducible if you purchased the book.
www.CrosswordBibleStudies.com

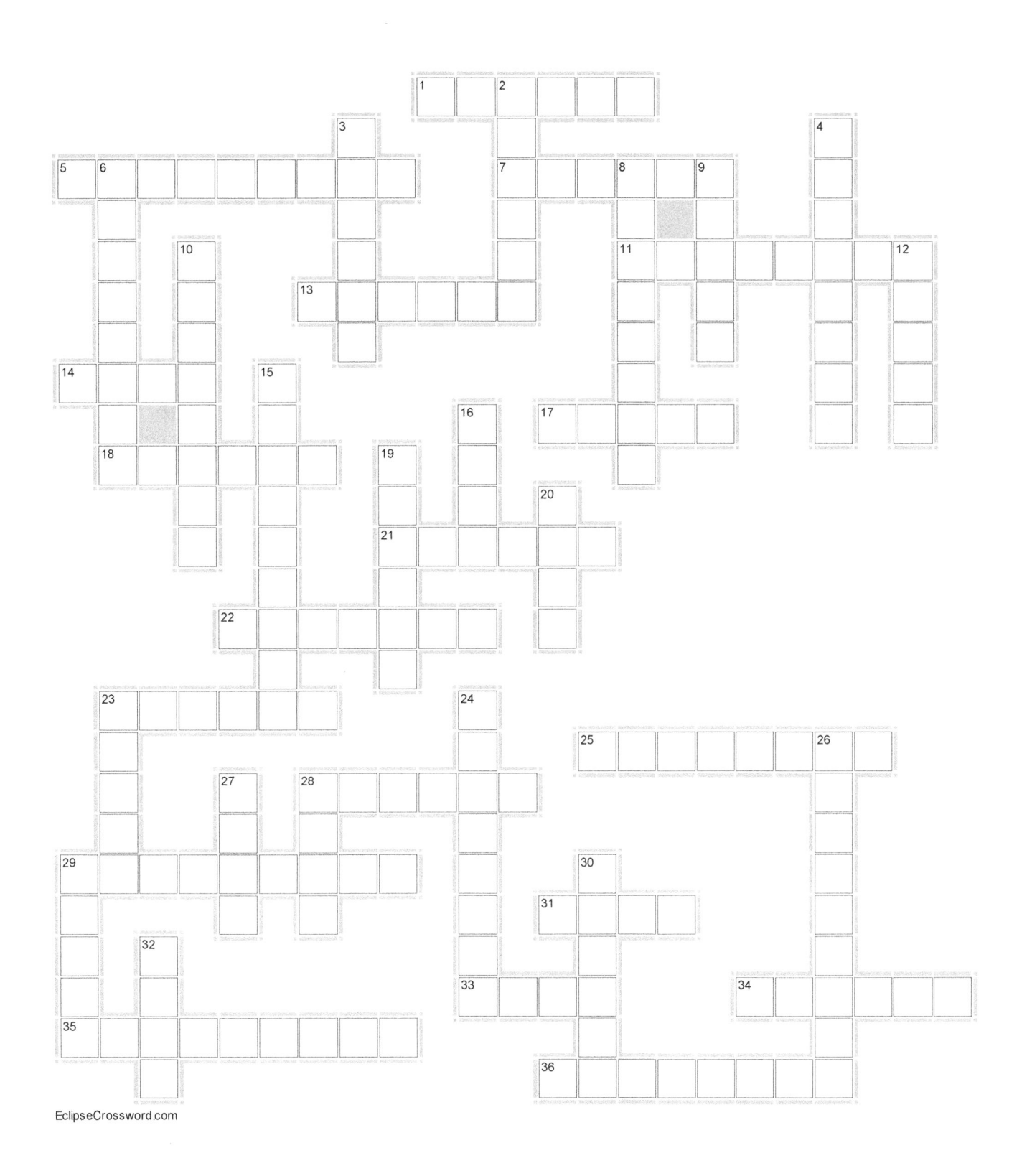

Psalm 18

Psalm 19

Across

4. the _____ of the LORD is pure (19:8)
7. rejoiceth as a strong man to run a _____ (19:5)
8. _____ also than honey and the honeycomb (19:10)
11. The fear of the LORD is clean, _____ for ever (19:9)
13. enlightening the _____ (19:8)
14. their words to the end of the _____ (19:4)
15. O LORD, my strength, and my _____ (19:14)
17. the _____ of the LORD is sure (19:7)
20. The statutes of the LORD are _____ (19:8)
21. In them hath he set a tabernacle for the _____ (19:4)
23. More to be _____ are they than gold, yea, than much fine gold (19:10)
27. Who can understand his _____? (19:12)
28. in keeping of them there is great _____ (19:11)
29. the _____ of my heart (19:14)
30. The law of the LORD is _____ (19:7)
31. Keep back thy _____ also from presumptuous sins (19:13)

Down

1. rejoicing the _____ (19:8)
2. The law of the LORD is perfect, converting the _____ (19:7)
3. Day unto day uttereth speech, and night unto night sheweth _____ (19:2)
5. The heavens _____ the glory of God; and the firmament sheweth his handywork (19:1)
6. There is no speech nor _____, where their voice is not heard (19:3)
9. the _____ of the LORD are true and righteous altogether (19:9)
10. cleanse thou me from _____ faults (19:12)
12. then shall I be _____, and I shall be innocent from the great transgression (19:13)
16. Moreover by them is thy servant _____ (19:11)
18. Let the words of my _____ (19:14)
19. making wise the _____ (19:7)
22. be _____ in thy sight, O LORD (19:14)
24. Their line is gone out through all the _____ (19:4)
25. let them not have _____ over me (19:13)
26. Which is as a _____ coming out of his chamber (19:5)

All Clues are taken directly from the 1611 edition of the King James Version (KJV).
Crossword Bible Studies: Top 40 Classic Songs in Psalms (KJV) © 2017 Christy Bower
These puzzles are reproducible if you purchased the book.
www.CrosswordBibleStudies.com

Psalm 19

Psalm 23

Across

1. beside the still _____ (23:2)
3. I shall not _____ (23:1)
6. The _____ is my shepherd (23:1)
7. in the _____ of the LORD for ever (23:6)
9. my _____ runneth over (23:5)
11. he leadeth me in the paths of _____ (23:3)
14. he leadeth me _____ the still waters (23:2)
15. follow me all the days of my _____ (23:6)
18. I will _____ no evil: for thou art with me (23:4)
19. and I will _____ in the house of the LORD for ever (23:6)
21. I walk through the _____ (23:4)
22. thou anointest my head with _____ (23:5)
23. thy rod and thy staff they _____ me (23:4)
24. Yea, though I _____ (23:4)
25. He maketh me to lie down in green _____ (23:2)

Down

2. thy rod and thy _____ (23:4)
4. Thou preparest a _____ before me (23:5)
5. Surely _____ and mercy (23:6)
8. The LORD is my _____ (23:1)
10. in the _____ of mine enemies (23:5)
12. He restoreth my _____ (23:3)
13. for his name's _____ (23:3)
16. shall _____ me all the days of my life (23:6)
17. the valley of the _____ of death (23:4)
20. in the presence of mine _____ (23:5)

All Clues are taken directly from the 1611 edition of the King James Version (KJV).
Crossword Bible Studies: Top 40 Classic Songs in Psalms (KJV) © 2017 Christy Bower
These puzzles are reproducible if you purchased the book.
www.CrosswordBibleStudies.com

Psalm 23

Psalm 24

Across

2. and _____ it upon the floods (24:2)
4. he is the King of glory. _____ (24:10)
5. hath not lifted up his soul unto vanity, nor sworn _____ (24:4)
6. that seek him, that _____ thy face (24:6)
8. This is the _____ of them that seek him (24:6)
10. and the King of glory shall _____ in (24:9)
12. Who is this _____ of glory? (24:8)
14. that seek thy _____ (24:6)
15. _____ up your heads, O ye gates (24:7)
16. Lift up your _____, O ye gates (24:9)
18. Who shall _____ into the hill of the Lord? (24:3)
19. _____ is this King of glory? (24:10)
21. who hath not lifted up his soul unto _____ (24:4)
22. Lift up your heads, O ye _____; even lift them up, ye everlasting doors (24:9)
23. Who is this King of glory? The Lord of _____ (24:10)
26. from the God of his _____ (24:5)
27. the _____, and they that dwell therein (24:1)

Down

1. the _____ from the Lord (24:5)
2. be ye lift up, ye _____ doors (24:7)
3. the Lord mighty in _____ (24:8)
7. He shall _____ the blessing (24:5)
9. and _____ from the God (24:5)
11. The Lord _____ and mighty (24:8)
13. The _____ is the Lord's, and the fulness thereof (24:1)
14. For he hath _____ it upon the seas (24:2)
17. or who shall _____ in his holy place? (24:3)
20. strong and _____ (24:8)
23. He that hath clean _____, and a pure heart (24:4)
24. he hath founded it upon the _____ (24:2)
25. the King of _____ shall come in (24:7)

All Clues are taken directly from the 1611 edition of the King James Version (KJV).
Crossword Bible Studies: Top 40 Classic Songs in Psalms (KJV) © 2017 Christy Bower
These puzzles are reproducible if you purchased the book.
www.CrosswordBibleStudies.com

Psalm 24

EclipseCrossword.com

All Clues are taken directly from the 1611 edition of the King James Version (KJV).
Crossword Bible Studies: Top 40 Classic Songs in Psalms (KJV) © 2017 Christy Bower
These puzzles are reproducible if you purchased the book.
www.CrosswordBibleStudies.com

Psalm 27

Across

2. believed to see the _____ of the Lord (27:13)
7. in the _____ of his tabernacle shall he hide me (27:5)
8. When my _____ and my mother (27:10)
10. of whom shall I be _____? (27:1)
11. For in the time of _____ (27:5)
14. When thou saidst, Seek ye my _____ (27:8)
15. _____ me not, neither forsake me, O God of my salvation (27:9)
17. they _____ and fell (27:2)
20. _____ me thy way, O Lord (27:11)
22. have _____ also upon me (27:7)
23. for false _____ are risen up against me (27:12)
24. in the land of the _____ (27:13)
25. Hear, O Lord, when I cry with my _____ (27:7)
26. When the _____, even mine enemies (27:2)
27. One thing have I _____ of the Lord (27:4)
31. _____ me not over unto the will of mine enemies (27:12)
33. be of good _____, and he shall strengthen thine heart: wait, I say, on the Lord (27:14)
36. have mercy also upon me, and _____ me (27:7)
37. my light and my _____ (27:1)
38. therefore will I offer in his tabernacle _____ of joy (27:6)
40. that I may _____ in the house of the Lord all the days of my life (27:4)
43. the Lord is the _____ of my life (27:1)
44. lead me in a plain _____, because of mine enemies (27:11)

Down

1. my _____ shall not fear (27:3)
3. desired of the Lord, that will I _____ after (27:4)
4. And now shall mine head be _____ up above mine enemies round about me (27:6)
5. whom shall I _____? (27:1)
6. witnesses are risen up against me, and such as breathe out _____ (27:12)
9. he shall _____ me in his pavilion (27:5)
12. to behold the _____ of the Lord (27:4)
13. thou hast been my _____ (27:9)
16. I had fainted, unless I had _____ (27:13)
18. and to enquire in his _____ (27:4)
19. I will sing, yea, I will sing _____ unto the Lord (27:6)
21. in this will I be _____ (27:3)
28. Hide not thy face far from me; put not thy _____ away in anger (27:9)
29. my father and my mother _____ me, then the Lord will take me up (27:10)
30. though _____ should rise against me (27:3)
32. mine _____ and my foes (27:2)
34. Though an _____ should encamp against me (27:3)
35. The Lord is my _____ (27:1)
39. he shall set me up upon a _____ (27:5)
41. _____ on the Lord (27:14)
42. my heart said unto thee, Thy face, _____, will I seek (27:8)

All Clues are taken directly from the 1611 edition of the King James Version (KJV).
Crossword Bible Studies: Top 40 Classic Songs in Psalms (KJV) © 2017 Christy Bower
These puzzles are reproducible if you purchased the book.
www.CrosswordBibleStudies.com

Psalm 27

All Clues are taken directly from the 1611 edition of the King James Version (KJV).
Crossword Bible Studies: Top 40 Classic Songs in Psalms (KJV) © 2017 Christy Bower
These puzzles are reproducible if you purchased the book.
www.CrosswordBibleStudies.com

Psalm 32

Across

3. When I kept _____, my bones waxed old through my roaring all the day long (32:3)
4. I will _____ thee with mine eye (32:8)
7. whose sin is _____ (32:1)
9. thy hand was _____ upon me (23:4)
10. I will _____ thee and teach thee in the way which thou shalt go (32:8)
12. For this shall every one that is godly _____ unto thee (32:6)
14. my moisture is turned into the drought of _____ (23:4)
16. I acknowledged my _____ unto thee, and mine iniquity have I not hid (32:5)
17. Blessed is he whose transgression is _____ (32:1)
20. shout for joy, all ye that are upright in _____ (32:11)
21. surely in the _____ of great waters they shall not come nigh unto him (32:6)
23. in whose _____ there is no guile (32:2)
25. pray unto thee in a time when thou mayest be _____ (32:6)
26. thou forgavest the _____ of my sin. Selah (32:5)

Down

1. as the mule, which have no _____ (32:9)
2. he that trusteth in the LORD, _____ shall compass him about (32:10)
5. _____, ye righteous: and shout for joy (32:11)
6. Be ye not as the _____, or as the mule (32:9)
8. thou shalt compass me about with songs of _____ (32:7)
11. thou shalt preserve me from _____ (32:7)
13. I said, I will _____ my transgressions unto the LORD (32:5)
15. Many _____ shall be to the wicked (32:10)
18. whose mouth must be held in with bit and _____, lest they come near unto thee (32:9)
19. _____ is the man unto whom the LORD imputeth not iniquity (32:2)
20. Thou art my _____ place (32:7)
22. For day and _____ (23:4)
24. Be glad in the _____ (32:11)

All Clues are taken directly from the 1611 edition of the King James Version (KJV).
Crossword Bible Studies: Top 40 Classic Songs in Psalms (KJV) © 2017 Christy Bower
These puzzles are reproducible if you purchased the book.
www.CrosswordBibleStudies.com

Psalm 32

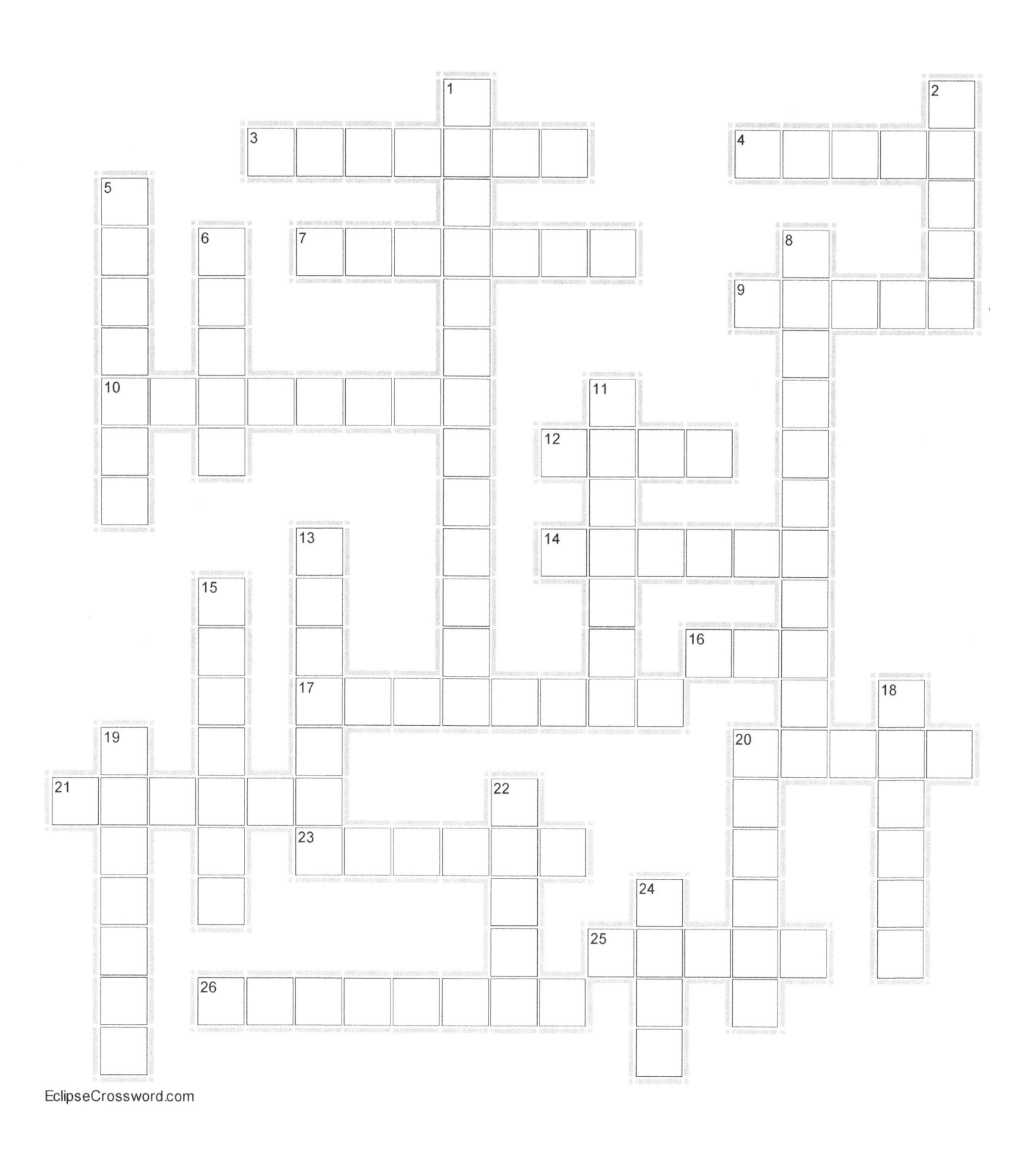

EclipseCrossword.com

All Clues are taken directly from the 1611 edition of the King James Version (KJV).
Crossword Bible Studies: Top 40 Classic Songs in Psalms (KJV) © 2017 Christy Bower
These puzzles are reproducible if you purchased the book.
www.CrosswordBibleStudies.com

Psalm 33

Across

1. For the _____ of the Lord is right (33:4)
7. all his works are done in _____ (33:4)
8. Let thy mercy, O Lord, be upon us, according as we _____ in thee (33:22)
9. let all the inhabitants of the world stand in _____ of him (33:8)
12. The Lord bringeth the _____ of the heathen to nought: he maketh the devices of the people of none effect (33:10)
14. to keep them alive in _____ (33:19)
15. For our heart shall rejoice in him, because we have _____ in his holy name (33:21)
17. Behold, the _____ of the Lord is upon them that fear him (33:18)
19. To deliver their soul from _____ (33:19)
20. Our soul waiteth for the Lord: he is our help and our _____ (33:20)
22. An horse is a vain thing for _____: neither shall he deliver any by his great strength (33:17)
25. Let all the earth _____ the Lord (33:8)
27. He fashioneth their _____ alike; he considereth all their works (33:15)
29. the people whom he hath chosen for his own _____ (33:12)
30. a _____ man is not delivered by much strength (33:16)

Down

2. _____ in the Lord, O ye righteous: for praise is comely for the upright (33:1)
3. He gathereth the _____ of the sea together as an heap: he layeth up the depth in storehouses (33:7)
4. From the place of his habitation he looketh upon all the _____ of the earth (33:14)
5. He loveth righteousness and judgment: the earth is full of the _____ of the Lord (33:5)
6. For he spake, and it was done; he _____, and it stood fast (33:9)
10. The counsel of the _____ standeth for ever, the thoughts of his heart to all generations (33:11)
11. There is no _____ saved by the multitude of an host (33:16)
13. play skilfully with a loud _____ (33:3)
16. By the word of the Lord were the heavens made; and all the host of them by the _____ of his mouth (33:6)
18. _____ is the nation whose God is the Lord (33:12)
21. sing unto him with the psaltery and an _____ of ten strings (33:2)
23. The Lord looketh from _____; he beholdeth all the sons of men (33:13)
24. _____ the Lord with harp (33:2)
26. upon them that fear him, upon them that hope in his _____ (33:18)
28. _____ unto him a new song (33:3)

Psalm 33

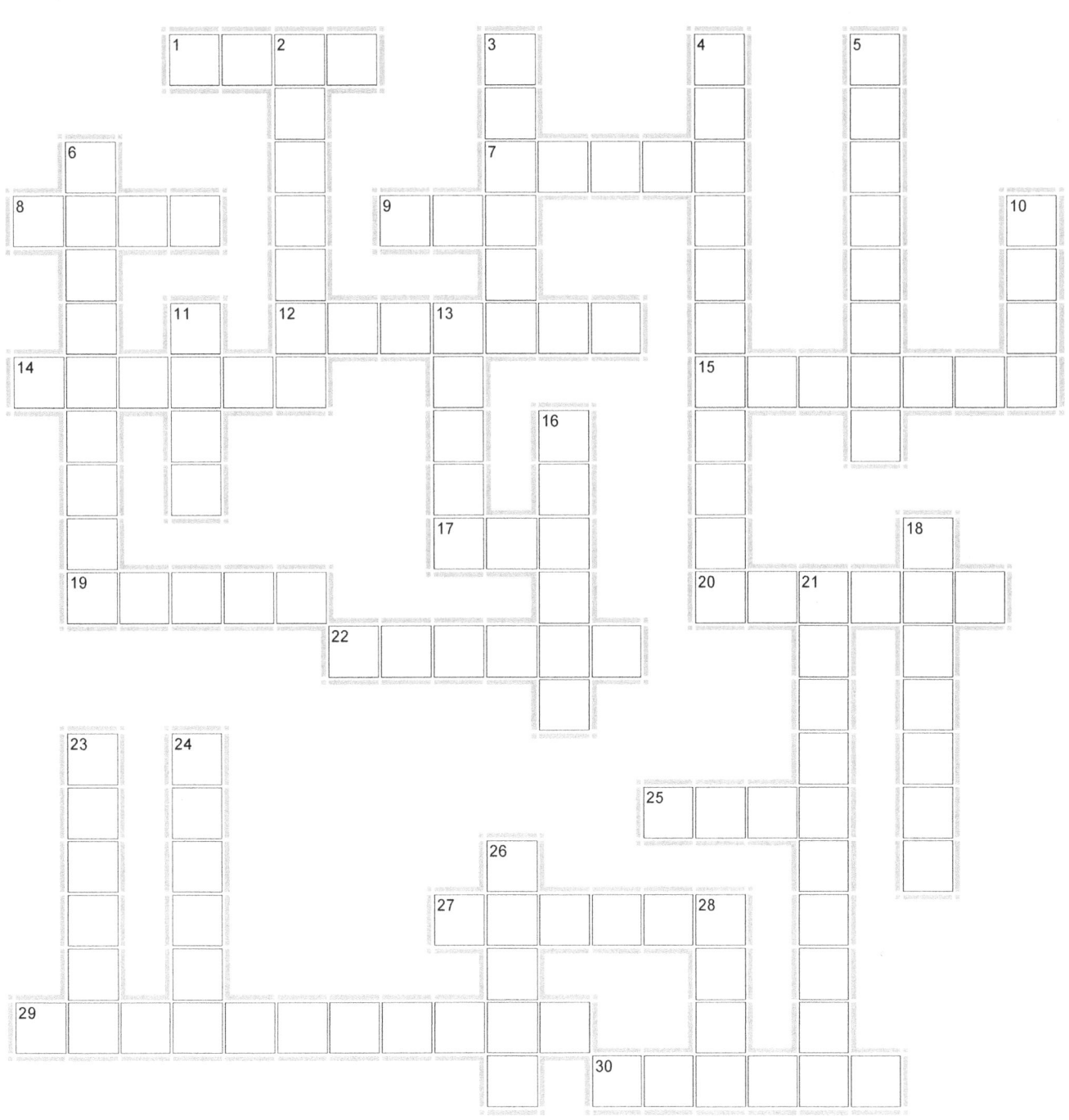

Psalm 34

Across

7. and saveth such as be of a _____ spirit (34:18)
9. the LORD is against them that do evil, to cut off the _____ of them from the earth (34:16)
11. _____ from evil, and do good; seek peace, and pursue it (34:14)
12. they that _____ the LORD shall not want any good thing (34:10)
15. and his _____ are open unto their cry (34:15)
19. This _____ man cried, and the LORD heard him (34:6)
20. _____ shall slay the wicked (34:21)
21. The _____ of the LORD encampeth round about them them (34:7)
23. the LORD heareth, and delivereth them out of all their _____ (34:17)
25. O fear the LORD, ye his _____ (34:9)
27. The _____ of the LORD is against them that do evil (34:16)
28. The righteous _____, and the LORD heareth (34:17)
30. but the _____ delivereth him out of them all (34:19)
31. they that hate the righteous shall be _____ (34:21)
35. hearken unto me: I will _____ you the fear of the LORD (34:11)
37. I sought the LORD, and he _____ me (34:4)
38. The LORD redeemeth the soul of his _____ (34:22)
39. The _____ of the LORD are upon the righteous (34:15)
40. The LORD is nigh unto them that are of a broken _____ (34:18)
42. Many are the _____ of the righteous (34:19)
43. O _____ and see that the LORD is good (34:8)

Down

1. The young lions do lack, and suffer _____ (34:10)
2. They _____ unto him, and were lightened (34:5)
3. not one of them is _____ (34:20)
4. Depart from evil, and do good; seek _____, and pursue it (34:14)
5. _____, ye children, hearken unto me (34:11)
6. the LORD encampeth round about them that _____ him, and delivereth them (34:7)
8. and thy lips from _____ guile (34:13)
10. I will _____ the LORD at all times (34:1)
13. he heard me, and _____ me from all my fears (34:4)
14. _____ thy tongue from evil (34:13)
16. the _____ shall hear thereof, and be glad (34:2)
17. his _____ shall continually be in my mouth (34:1)
18. O _____ the LORD with me (34:3)
22. My soul shall make her _____ in the LORD (34:2)
24. He keepeth all his _____ (34:20)
26. none of them that _____ in him shall be desolate (34:22)
29. The eyes of the LORD are upon the _____ (34:15)
32. and let us _____ his name together (34:3)
33. the LORD heard him, and _____ him out of all his troubles (34:6)
34. _____ is the man that trusteth in him (34:8)
36. their faces were not _____ (34:5)
41. What man is he that desireth _____, and loveth many days, that he may see good? (34:12)

All Clues are taken directly from the 1611 edition of the King James Version (KJV).
Crossword Bible Studies: Top 40 Classic Songs in Psalms (KJV) © 2017 Christy Bower
These puzzles are reproducible if you purchased the book.
www.CrosswordBibleStudies.com

Psalm 34

Psalm 37

Across

1. The mouth of the righteous speaketh _____, and his tongue talketh of judgment (37:30)
2. _____ from evil, and do good; and dwell for evermore (37:27)
4. The LORD knoweth the days of the upright: and their _____ shall be for ever (37:18)
9. Mark the perfect man, and behold the upright: for the end of that man is _____ (37:37)
10. _____ thyself also in the LORD; and he shall give thee the desires of thine heart (37:4)
13. The wicked borroweth, and payeth not again: but the righteous sheweth _____, and giveth (37:21)
14. shall delight themselves in the _____ of peace (37:11)
16. And the LORD shall _____ them, and deliver them (37:40)
18. He is ever _____, and lendeth; and his seed is blessed (37:26)
20. Though he fall, he shall not be utterly cast down: for the LORD upholdeth him with his _____ (37:24)
22. _____ in the LORD, and wait patiently for him: fret not thyself because of him who prospereth in his way, because of the man who bringeth wicked devices to pass (37:7)
23. For such as be blessed of him shall _____ the earth; and they that be cursed of him shall be cut off (37:22)
25. The _____ of his God is in his heart; none of his steps shall slide (37:31)
26. The Lord shall _____ at him: for he seeth that his day is coming (37:13)
27. For yet a little while, and the _____ shall not be: yea, thou shalt diligently consider his place, and it shall not be (37:10)
28. For the arms of the wicked shall be broken: but the LORD upholdeth the _____ (37:17)
30. _____ in the LORD, and do good; so shalt thou dwell in the land, and verily thou shalt be fed (37:3)
31. Yet he passed away, and, lo, he was not: yea, I sought him, but he could not be _____ (37:36)
32. I have seen the wicked in great _____, and spreading himself like a green bay tree (37:35)
33. _____ from anger, and forsake wrath: fret not thyself in any wise to do evil (37:8)

Down

1. _____ on the LORD, and keep his way, and he shall exalt thee to inherit the land: when the wicked are cut off, thou shalt see it (37:34)
3. They shall not be _____ in the evil time: and in the days of famine they shall be satisfied (37:19)
5. The wicked have drawn out the sword, and have bent their bow, to cast down the poor and _____, and to slay such as be of upright conversation (37:14)
6. he shall _____ them from the wicked, and save them, because they trust in him (37:40)
7. But the _____ shall inherit the earth (37:11)
8. I have been young, and now am old; yet have I not seen the righteous _____, nor his seed begging bread (37:25)
11. For evildoers shall be cut off: but those that wait upon the _____, they shall inherit the earth (37:9)
12. the LORD: he is their strength in the time of _____ (37:39)
15. _____ thy way unto the LORD; trust also in him; and he shall bring it to pass (37:5)
17. For they shall soon be cut down like the _____, and wither as the green herb (37:2)
19. But the _____ of the righteous is of the LORD (37:39)
21. And he shall bring forth thy righteousness as the _____, and thy judgment as the noonday (37:6)
22. A little that a righteous man hath is better than the _____ of many wicked (37:16)
24. neither be thou _____ against the workers of iniquity (37:1)
29. The _____ of a good man are ordered by the LORD: and he delighteth in his way (37:23)
31. _____ not thyself because of evildoers (37:1)

All Clues are taken directly from the 1611 edition of the King James Version (KJV).
Crossword Bible Studies: Top 40 Classic Songs in Psalms (KJV) © 2017 Christy Bower
These puzzles are reproducible if you purchased the book.
www.CrosswordBibleStudies.com

Psalm 37

Psalm 40

Across

1. in the volume of the book it is _____ of me (40:7)
2. a new song in my mouth, even _____ unto our God (40:3)
11. they are more than the _____ of mine head: therefore my heart faileth me (40:12)
12. say continually, The LORD be _____ (40:16)
13. _____ and offering thou didst not desire; mine ears hast thou opened (40:6)
15. he inclined unto me, and _____ my cry (40:1)
18. He brought me up also out of an _____ pit, out of the miry clay (40:2)
19. And he hath put a new _____ in my mouth (40:3)
20. Then said I, Lo, I come: in the _____ of the book (40:7)
21. I have declared thy _____ and thy salvation (40:10)
23. and thy _____ which are to us-ward: they cannot be reckoned up in order unto thee (40:5)
24. they are more than can be _____ (40:5)
31. if I would _____ and speak of them (40:5)
32. _____ is that man that maketh the LORD his trust (40:4)
33. let such as love thy _____ say continually (40:16)
34. I have _____ righteousness in the great congregation (40:9)
35. have not concealed thy lovingkindness and thy truth from the great _____ (40:10)
36. burnt offering and sin offering hast thou not _____ (40:6)
37. Let them be desolate for a _____ of their shame that say unto me, Aha, aha (40:15)

Down

1. Many, O LORD my God, are thy _____ works which thou hast done (40:5)
3. out of the miry clay, and set my feet upon a _____, and established my goings (40:2)
4. For innumerable evils have compassed me about: mine _____ have taken hold upon me, so that I am not able to look up (40:12)
5. Let them be ashamed and _____ together that seek after my soul to destroy it (40:14)
6. I have not concealed thy _____ and thy truth (40:10)
7. I have not hid thy _____ within my heart (40:10)
8. many shall see it, and fear, and shall _____ in the LORD (40:3)
9. I _____ patiently for the LORD (40:1)
10. thou art my help and my _____; make no tarrying, O my God (40:17)
14. O LORD, make _____ to help me (40:13)
16. Be _____, O LORD, to deliver me (40:13)
17. and respecteth not the _____, nor such as turn aside to lies (40:4)
18. yea, thy law is within my _____ (40:8)
22. But I am poor and _____; yet the Lord thinketh upon me (40:17)
25. Withhold not thou thy tender _____ from me, O LORD (40:11)
26. I _____ to do thy will, O my God (40:8)
27. let thy lovingkindness and thy truth continually _____ me (40:11)
28. let them be driven _____ and put to shame that wish me evil (40:14)
29. Let all those that seek thee _____ and be glad in thee magnified (40:16)
30. lo, I have not _____ my lips, O LORD, thou knowest (40:9)

All Clues are taken directly from the 1611 edition of the King James Version (KJV).
Crossword Bible Studies: Top 40 Classic Songs in Psalms (KJV) © 2017 Christy Bower
These puzzles are reproducible if you purchased the book.
www.CrosswordBibleStudies.com

Psalm 40

Psalm 42

Across

3. _____ thou in God: for I shall yet praise him (43:11)
4. Deep calleth unto _____ (43:7)
6. I had gone with the _____, I went with them to the house of God (43:4)
8. When I remember these things, I _____ out my soul in me (43:4)
11. day and _____ (42:3)
12. hope thou in God: for I shall yet _____ him for the help of his countenance (43:5)
13. _____ art thou cast down, O my soul? (43:11)
14. As the hart panteth after the water brooks, so panteth my soul after thee, O _____ (42:1)
15. for I shall yet praise him, who is the _____ of my countenance, and my God (43:11)
17. I will say unto God my _____ (43:9)
18. my _____ unto the God of my life (43:8)
20. I went with them to the house of God, with the _____ of joy and praise, with a multitude that kept holyday (43:4)
22. in the night his _____ shall be with me (43:8)
23. why art thou _____ in me? hope thou in God (43:5)
24. why go I mourning because of the oppression of the _____? (43:9)

Down

1. O my God, my soul is cast down within me: therefore will I _____ thee from the land of Jordan, and of the Hermonites, from the hill Mizar (43:6)
2. My soul thirsteth for God, for the _____ God (42:2)
4. Yet the LORD will command his lovingkindness in the _____, and in the night (43:8)
5. when shall I come and _____ before God? (42:2)
7. they say _____ unto me, Where is thy God? (43:10)
9. As with a sword in my bones, mine enemies _____ me (43:10)
10. they continually say unto me, _____ is thy God? (42:3)
13. at the noise of thy _____ (43:7)
16. Why hast thou _____ me? (43:9)
19. all thy _____ and thy billows are gone over me (43:7)
21. Why art thou cast down, O my _____? (43:5)

All Clues are taken directly from the 1611 edition of the King James Version (KJV).
Crossword Bible Studies: Top 40 Classic Songs in Psalms (KJV) © 2017 Christy Bower
These puzzles are reproducible if you purchased the book.
www.CrosswordBibleStudies.com

Psalm 42

Psalm 46

Across

2. he burneth the _____ in the fire (46:9)
8. I will be _____ in the earth (46:10)
9. _____ is our refuge and strength (46:1)
11. a very present help in _____ (46:1)
12. the works of the LORD, what _____ he hath made in the earth (46:8)
16. the _____ place of the tabernacles of the most High (46:4)
17. The LORD of _____ is with us (46:7)
19. a very _____ help in trouble (46:1)
21. he uttered his _____, the earth melted (46:6)
22. I will be exalted among the _____ (46:10)
28. Therefore will not we _____, though the earth be removed (46:2)
30. He maketh _____ to cease unto the end of the earth (46:9)
32. God is our refuge and _____ (46:1)
33. though the mountains _____ with the swelling thereof. Selah (46:3)

Down

1. There is a _____, the streams whereof shall make glad the city of God (46:4)
3. Though the _____ thereof roar and be troubled (46:3)
4. God is in the _____ of her (46:5)
5. the God of _____ is our refuge (46:7)
6. The heathen _____, the kingdoms were moved (46:6)
7. Be _____, and know that I am God (46:10)
10. the tabernacles of the _____ High (46:4)
13. the God of Jacob is our refuge. _____ (46:7)
14. _____, behold the works of the LORD (46:8)
15. and though the _____ be carried into the midst of the sea (46:2)
18. he breaketh the bow, and cutteth the _____ in sunder (46:9)
20. the _____ were moved (46:6)
23. God shall _____ her, and that right early (46:5)
24. the God of Jacob is our _____ (46:11)
25. behold the _____ of the LORD (46:8)
26. though the _____ be removed (46:2)
27. she shall not be _____ (46:5)
29. The _____ of hosts is with us (46:11)
31. the streams whereof shall make _____ the city of God (46:4)

All Clues are taken directly from the 1611 edition of the King James Version (KJV).

Crossword Bible Studies: Top 40 Classic Songs in Psalms (KJV) © 2017 Christy Bower

These puzzles are reproducible if you purchased the book.

www.CrosswordBibleStudies.com

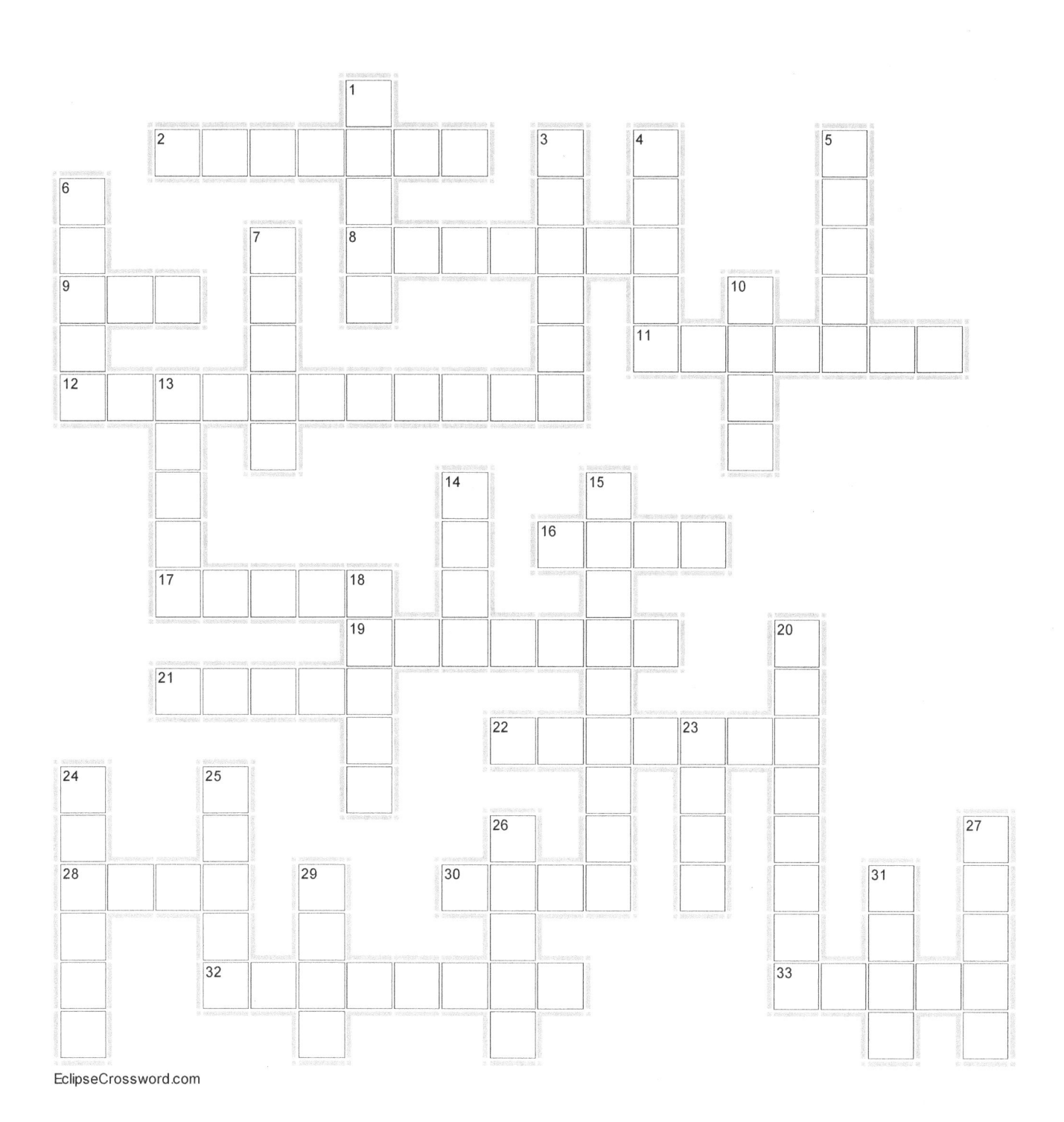

Psalm 46

Psalm 50

Across

4. Gather my _____ together unto me; those that have made a covenant with me by sacrifice (50:5)
8. to him that ordereth his conversation aright will I shew the _____ of God (50:23)
9. Our God shall _____, and shall not keep silence (50:3)
10. Whoso offereth praise glorifieth me: and to him that ordereth his _____ aright (50:23)
12. And call upon me in the day of _____: I will deliver thee (50:15)
13. Offer unto God _____; and pay thy vows unto the most High (50:14)
16. When thou sawest a thief, then thou consentedst with him, and hast been _____ with adulterers (50:18)
20. Thou sittest and speakest against thy _____; thou slanderest thine own mother's son (50:20)
21. Now consider this, ye that _____ God, lest I tear you in pieces, and there be none to deliver (50:22)
22. for the _____ is mine, and the fulness thereof (50:12)
23. Will I eat the _____ of bulls, or drink the blood of goats? (50:13)
27. These things hast thou done, and I kept _____; thou thoughtest that I was altogether such an one as thyself (50:21)
29. And the heavens shall declare his _____ (50:6)
30. The _____ God, even the LORD, hath spoken (50:1)

Down

1. Out of _____, the perfection of beauty, God hath shined (50:2)
2. For every beast of the forest is mine, and the _____ upon a thousand hills (50:10)
3. the LORD, hath spoken, and called the earth from the _____ of the sun unto the going down thereof (50:1)
5. I will not reprove thee for thy _____ or thy burnt offerings, to have been continually before me (50:8)
6. _____, O my people, and I will speak; O Israel, and I will testify against thee: I am God, even thy God (50:7)
7. But unto the _____ God saith, What hast thou to do to declare my statutes, or that thou shouldest take my covenant in thy mouth? (50:16)
11. Seeing thou hatest _____, and castest my words behind thee (50:17)
14. I will deliver thee, and thou shalt _____ me (50:15)
15. I know all the fowls of the _____: and the wild beasts of the field are mine (50:11)
17. thou thoughtest that I was altogether such an one as thyself: but I will _____ thee, and set them in order before thine eyes (50:21)
18. a _____ shall devour before him, and it shall be very tempestuous round about him (50:3)
19. for God is _____ himself. Selah (50:6)
24. If I were _____, I would not tell thee (50:12)
25. He shall call to the _____ from above, and to the earth, that he may judge his people (50:4)
26. I will take no bullock out of thy _____, nor he goats out of thy folds (50:9)
28. Thou givest thy _____ to evil, and thy tongue frameth deceit (50:19)

Psalm 50

Psalm 51

Across

3. Behold, thou desirest _____ in the inward parts (51:6)
5. Then shalt thou be _____ with the sacrifices of righteousness (51:19)
6. For I _____ my transgressions: and my sin is ever before me (51:3)
10. _____ me with thy free spirit (51:12)
11. _____ me from bloodguiltiness, O God (51:14)
12. _____ out my transgressions (51:1)
14. a broken and a _____ heart, O God, thou wilt not despise (51:17)
16. wash me, and I shall be whiter than _____ (51:7)
17. _____ in me a clean heart, O God (51:10)
18. _____ me throughly from mine iniquity (51:2)
20. that the bones which thou hast broken may _____ (51:8)
21. For thou desirest not _____; else would I give it (51:16)
24. Hide thy _____ from my sins (51:9)
27. O Lord, open thou my lips; and my _____ shall shew forth thy praise (51:15)
29. Against thee, thee only, have I _____, and done this evil in thy sight (51:4)
30. O God, thou God of my _____ (51:14)
31. Cast me not away from thy _____ (51:11)

Down

1. according unto the _____ of thy tender mercies (51:1)
2. Then will I _____ transgressors thy ways (51:13)
4. _____ renew a right spirit within me (51:10)
7. Make me to hear joy and _____ (51:8)
8. take not thy holy _____ from me (51:11)
9. Have _____ upon me, O God, according to thy lovingkindness (51:1)
12. The sacrifices of God are a _____ spirit (51:17)
13. my _____ shall sing aloud of thy righteousness (51:14)
15. _____ unto me the joy of thy salvation (51:12)
17. _____ me from my sin (51:2)
19. in the hidden part thou shalt make me to know _____ (51:6)
22. blot out all mine _____ (51:9)
23. thou delightest not in burnt _____ (51:16)
25. sinners shall be _____ unto thee (51:13)
26. Do good in thy good pleasure unto Zion: build thou the walls of _____ (51:18)
28. Purge me with _____, and I shall be clean (51:7)

All Clues are taken directly from the 1611 edition of the King James Version (KJV).
Crossword Bible Studies: Top 40 Classic Songs in Psalms (KJV) © 2017 Christy Bower
These puzzles are reproducible if you purchased the book.
www.CrosswordBibleStudies.com

Psalm 51

Psalm 56

Across

2. put thou my tears into thy _____ (56:8)
4. all their _____ are against me for evil (56:5)
6. that I may _____ before God in the light of the living? (56:13)
8. Be _____ unto me, O God (56:1)
11. What time I am _____, I will trust in thee (56:3)
12. for man would _____ me up; he fighting daily oppresseth me (56:1)
14. In God have I put my _____: I will not be afraid (56:11)
15. this I _____; for God is for me (56:9)
18. in thine _____ cast down the people, O God (56:7)
19. When I _____ unto thee, then shall mine enemies turn back (56:9)
22. I will not be afraid what _____ can do unto me (56:11)
24. In _____ I will praise his word, in God I have put my trust (56:4)
25. Shall they _____ by iniquity? (56:7)
26. Mine _____ would daily swallow me up (56:2)

Down

1. Thy _____ are upon me, O God (56:12)
3. put thou my tears into thy bottle: are they not in thy _____? (56:8)
5. They gather themselves together, they _____ themselves (56:6)
6. Every day they wrest my _____ (56:5)
7. In God will I praise his _____ (56:10)
9. wilt not thou deliver my feet from _____, that I may walk before God (56:13)
10. for they be many that _____ against me, O thou most High (56:2)
13. Thou tellest my _____ (56:8)
14. They gather themselves _____ (56:6)
16. they mark my steps, when they _____ for my soul (56:6)
17. in the Lord will I _____ his word (56:10)
20. I will _____ praises unto thee (56:12)
21. For thou hast delivered my soul from _____ (56:13)
23. I will not _____ what flesh can do unto me (56:4)

All Clues are taken directly from the 1611 edition of the King James Version (KJV).
Crossword Bible Studies: Top 40 Classic Songs in Psalms (KJV) © 2017 Christy Bower
These puzzles are reproducible if you purchased the book.
www.CrosswordBibleStudies.com

Psalm 56

Psalm 62

Across

4. they _____ in lies (62:4)
6. How long will ye imagine _____ against a man? (62:3)
7. the rock of my _____, and my refuge, is in God (62:7)
10. thou renderest to every man according to his _____ (62:12)
14. Truly my _____ waiteth upon God: from him cometh my salvation (62:1)
15. for my _____ is from him (62:5)
16. He only is my _____ and my salvation (62:2)
17. Surely men of low degree are _____ (62:9)
22. God hath _____ once; twice have I heard this; (62:11)
23. they _____ with their mouth (62:4)
24. they bless with their mouth, but they _____ inwardly (62:4)
25. that _____ belongeth unto God (62:11)

Down

1. Trust not in _____, and become not vain in robbery (62:10)
2. ye people, pour out your _____ before him (62:8)
3. They only consult to _____ him down from his excellency (62:4)
5. men of high _____ are a lie (62:9)
8. God is a refuge for us. _____ (62:8)
9. He only is my rock and my _____ (62:6)
11. My soul, _____ thou only upon God (62:5)
12. Also unto thee, O Lord, belongeth _____ (62:12)
13. if riches _____, set not your heart upon them (62:10)
18. _____ in him at all times (62:8)
19. God is a _____ for us (62:8)
20. he is my defence; I shall not be greatly _____ (62:2)
21. In God is my salvation and my _____ (62:7)

All Clues are taken directly from the 1611 edition of the King James Version (KJV).
Crossword Bible Studies: Top 40 Classic Songs in Psalms (KJV) © 2017 Christy Bower
These puzzles are reproducible if you purchased the book.
www.CrosswordBibleStudies.com

Psalm 62

Psalm 63

Across

2. shall go into the lower parts of the _____ (63:9)
4. My _____ followeth hard after thee (63:8)
5. my _____ shall praise thee (63:5)
8. O _____, thou art my God (63:1)
9. as I have seen thee in the _____ (63:2)
10. meditate on thee in the night _____ (63:6)
13. Because thy lovingkindness is better than _____ (63:3)
14. praise thee with _____ lips (63:5)
16. But the _____ shall rejoice in God; every one that sweareth by him shall glory (63:11)
17. But those that seek my soul, to _____ it (63:9)
19. in a dry and _____ land, where no water is (63:1)
21. Because thou hast been my _____ (63:7)
24. remember thee upon my bed, and _____ on thee (63:6)

Down

1. Thus will I _____ thee while I live (63:4)
3. thy _____ hand upholdeth me (63:8)
4. therefore in the _____ of thy wings will I rejoice (63:7)
6. my lips shall _____ thee (63:3)
7. My soul shall be _____ as with marrow and fatness (63:5)
8. to see thy power and thy _____ (63:2)
11. I will lift up my _____ in thy name (63:4)
12. thou art my God; _____ will I seek thee (63:1)
15. my soul thirsteth for thee, my _____ longeth for thee (63:1)
18. when I _____ thee upon my bed (63:6)
20. They shall fall by the _____ (63:10)
22. the mouth of them that _____ lies shall be stopped (63:11)
23. they shall be a portion for _____ (63:10)

All Clues are taken directly from the 1611 edition of the King James Version (KJV).
Crossword Bible Studies: Top 40 Classic Songs in Psalms (KJV) © 2017 Christy Bower
These puzzles are reproducible if you purchased the book.
www.CrosswordBibleStudies.com

Psalm 63

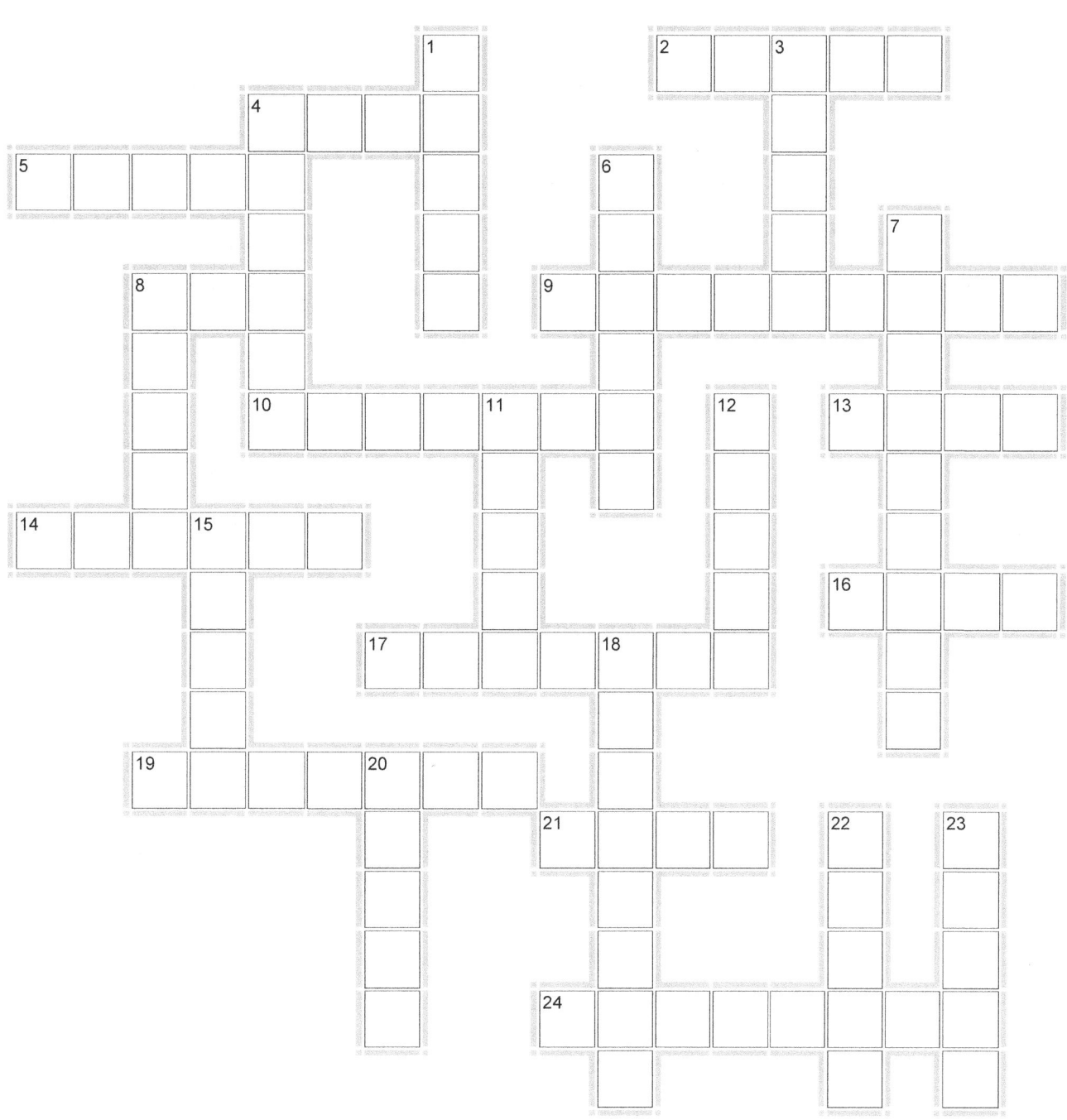

Psalm 67

Across

2. for thou shalt _____ the people (67:4)
5. may be _____ upon earth (67:2)
8. the ends of the earth shall _____ him (67:7)
9. be _____ unto us, and bless us (67:1)
10. That thy _____ may be known (67:2)
12. and cause his face to _____ upon us; Selah (67:1)
14. _____ the people praise thee, O God (67:5)
15. Let the _____ praise thee, O God (67:3)
16. let all the people _____ thee (67:3)
20. _____ be merciful (67:1)
21. Then shall the earth _____ her increase (67:6)
22. O let the nations be _____ (67:4)
23. nations be glad and _____ for joy (67:4)

Down

1. and God, even _____ own God, shall bless us (67:6)
3. and _____ the nations upon earth (67:4)
4. Then shall the earth yield her _____ (67:6)
6. and govern the nations upon earth. _____ (67:4)
7. thou shalt judge the people _____ (67:4)
8. and cause his _____ to shine upon us; Selah (67:1)
11. God be merciful unto us, and _____ us (67:1)
13. thy saving health among all _____ (67:2)
17. let _____ the people praise thee (67:3)
18. may be known upon _____ (67:2)
19. all the _____ of the earth (67:7)

All Clues are taken directly from the 1611 edition of the King James Version (KJV).
Crossword Bible Studies: Top 40 Classic Songs in Psalms (KJV) © 2017 Christy Bower
These puzzles are reproducible if you purchased the book.
www.CrosswordBibleStudies.com

Psalm 67

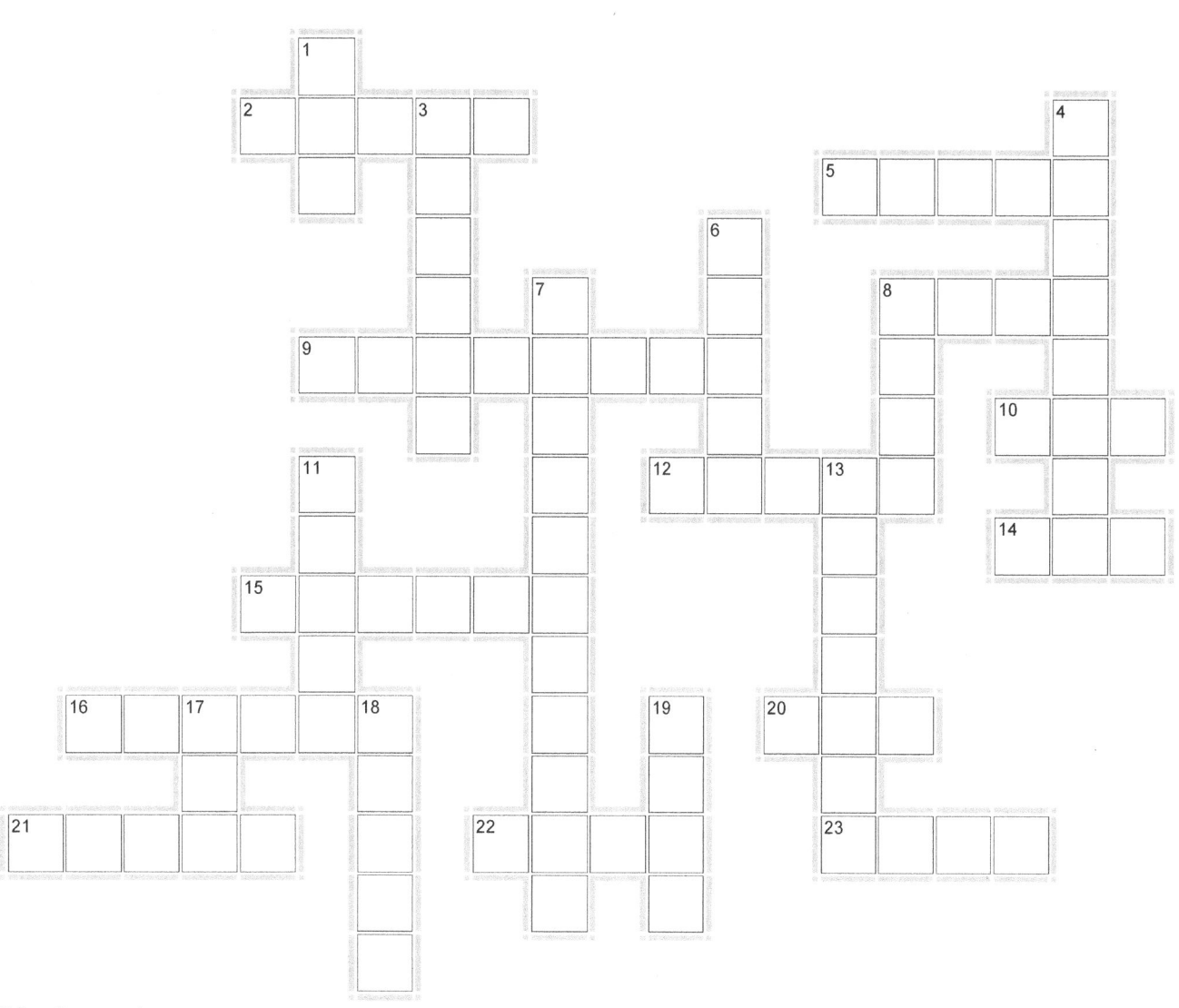

Psalm 73

Across

1. Surely thou didst set them in _____ places: thou castedst them down into destruction (73:18)
4. How are they brought into _____, as in a moment! they are utterly consumed with terrors (73:19)
7. As a _____ when one awaketh; so, O Lord, when thou awakest, thou shalt despise their image (73:20)
10. Whom have I in _____ but thee? (73:25)
14. They are corrupt, and speak wickedly concerning _____: they speak loftily (73:8)
15. until I went into the _____ of God; then understood I their end (73:17)
17. They set their _____ against the heavens, and their tongue walketh through the earth (73:9)
20. Nevertheless I am continually with thee: thou hast holden me by my right _____ (73:23)
21. My flesh and my heart faileth: but God is the strength of my heart, and my _____ for ever (73:26)
24. But it is good for me to draw near to God: I have put my trust in the Lord God, that I may _____ all thy works (73:28)
26. For there are no bands in their death: but their _____ is firm (73:4)
28. For I was _____ at the foolish, when I saw the prosperity of the wicked (73:3)
29. But it is good for me to draw _____ to God (73:28)
30. Thus my heart was _____, and I was pricked in my reins (73:21)

Down

2. Therefore his _____ return hither: and waters of a full cup are wrung out to them (73:10)
3. Truly God is good to Israel, even to such as are of a _____ heart (73:1)
5. But as for me, my feet were almost gone; my steps had well nigh _____ (73:2)
6. Behold, these are the ungodly, who _____ in the world; they increase in riches (73:12)
8. For, lo, they that are far from thee shall _____: thou hast destroyed all them that go a whoring from thee (73:27)
9. Therefore _____ compasseth them about as a chain; violence covereth them as a garment (73:6)
11. Verily I have cleansed my heart in _____, and washed my hands in innocency (73:13)
12. So foolish was I, and ignorant: I was as a _____ before thee (73:22)
13. And they say, How doth God know? and is there _____ in the most High? (73:11)
16. I have put my _____ in the Lord God, that I may declare all thy works (73:28)
18. Thou shalt _____ me with thy counsel, and afterward receive me to glory (73:24)
19. For all the day long have I been plagued, and _____ every morning (73:14)
21. When I thought to know this, it was too _____ for me (73:16)
22. If I say, I will speak thus; behold, I should _____ against the generation of thy children (73:15)
23. and there is none upon earth that I _____ beside thee (73:25)
25. They are not in _____ as other men; neither are they plagued like other men (73:5)
27. Their eyes stand out with fatness: they have more than heart could _____ (73:7)

All Clues are taken directly from the 1611 edition of the King James Version (KJV).
Crossword Bible Studies: Top 40 Classic Songs in Psalms (KJV) © 2017 Christy Bower
These puzzles are reproducible if you purchased the book.
www.CrosswordBibleStudies.com

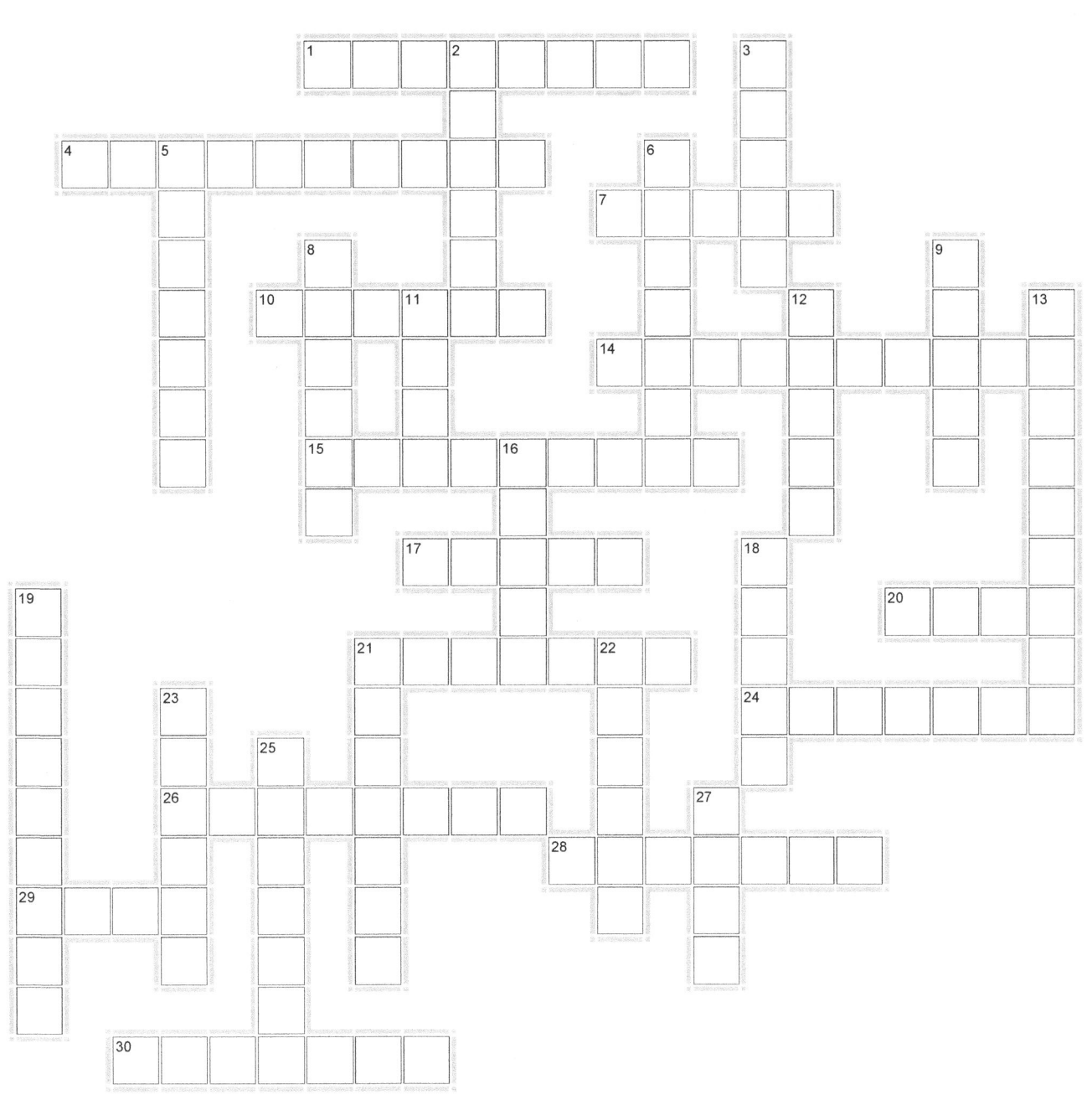

Psalm 73

All Clues are taken directly from the 1611 edition of the King James Version (KJV).
Crossword Bible Studies: Top 40 Classic Songs in Psalms (KJV) © 2017 Christy Bower
These puzzles are reproducible if you purchased the book.
www.CrosswordBibleStudies.com

Psalm 84

Across

2. rather be a doorkeeper in the house of my God, than to dwell in the tents of _____ (84:10)
4. the _____ also filleth the pools (94:6)
5. O Lord God of hosts, hear my _____ (84:8)
9. they will be still praising thee. _____ (84:4)
10. They go from strength to strength, every one of them in _____ appeareth before God (84:7)
14. they will be still _____ thee (84:4)
15. in whose _____ are the ways of them (84:5)
16. hear my prayer: give _____, O God of Jacob. Selah (84:8)
17. How _____ are thy tabernacles (84:1)
18. my heart and my _____ crieth out (84:2)
21. O Lord of _____ (84:12)
23. _____ is the man that trusteth in thee (84:12)
26. Who passing through the valley of Baca make it a _____ (94:6)
27. My _____ longeth, yea, even fainteth (84:2)
28. fainteth for the _____ of the Lord (84:2)
30. where she may lay her young, even thine _____ (84:3)
31. no _____ thing will he withhold from them that walk uprightly (84:11)

Down

1. the Lord will give _____ and glory (84:11)
3. Blessed is the man whose _____ is in thee (84:5)
6. the swallow a nest for herself, where she may lay her _____ (84:3)
7. How amiable are thy _____, O Lord of hosts! (84:1)
8. I had rather be a _____ in the house of my God (84:10)
9. Yea, the _____ hath found an house, and the swallow a nest for herself (84:3)
11. O Lord of hosts, my _____, and my God (84:3)
12. For a day in thy courts is better than a _____ (84:10)
13. look upon the face of thine _____ (84:9)
19. that dwell in thy _____ (84:4)
20. Behold, O God our _____ (84:9)
22. the sparrow hath found an house, and the _____ a nest for herself (84:3)
24. my flesh crieth out for the _____ God (84:2)
25. Blessed are they that _____ in thy house (84:4)
29. For the Lord God is a _____ and shield (84:11)

All Clues are taken directly from the 1611 edition of the King James Version (KJV).
Crossword Bible Studies: Top 40 Classic Songs in Psalms (KJV) © 2017 Christy Bower
These puzzles are reproducible if you purchased the book.
www.CrosswordBibleStudies.com

Psalm 84

Psalm 91

Across

2. Thou shalt _____ upon the lion and adder (91:13)
7. He shall cover thee with his _____ (91:4)
8. the most High, thy _____ (91:9)
9. my God; in him will I _____ (91:2)
13. nor for the _____ that wasteth at noonday (91:6)
15. I will _____ him, and honour him (91:15)
16. Because he hath set his _____ upon me, therefore will I deliver him (91:14)
17. his truth shall be thy _____ and buckler (91:4)
19. shall abide under the shadow of the _____ (91:1)
20. I will be with him in _____ (91:15)
21. under his _____ shalt thou trust (91:4)
24. For he shall give his _____ charge over thee, to keep thee in all thy ways (91:11)
25. He that dwelleth in the _____ place of the most High (91:1)
26. Because thou hast made the LORD, which is my _____ (91:9)
27. for the terror by night; nor for the _____ that flieth by day (91:5)

Down

1. They shall bear thee up in their _____ (91:12)
3. Thou shalt not be _____ for the terror by night (91:5)
4. the young lion and the dragon shalt thou _____ under feet (91:13)
5. A _____ shall fall at thy side, and ten thousand at thy right hand; but it shall not come nigh thee (91:7)
6. lest thou dash thy _____ against a stone (91:12)
10. With long life will I _____ him (91:16)
11. Only with thine eyes shalt thou behold and see the reward of the _____ (91:8)
12. I satisfy him, and shew him my _____ (91:16)
13. There shall no evil befall thee, neither shall any plague come nigh thy _____ (91:10)
14. I will say of the LORD, He is my refuge and my _____ (91:2)
18. Nor for the pestilence that walketh in _____ (91:6)
22. Surely he shall deliver thee from the _____ of the fowler (91:3)
23. I will set him on high, because he hath known my _____ (91:14)
24. He shall call upon me, and I will _____ him (91:15)

All Clues are taken directly from the 1611 edition of the King James Version (KJV).
Crossword Bible Studies: Top 40 Classic Songs in Psalms (KJV) © 2017 Christy Bower
These puzzles are reproducible if you purchased the book.
www.CrosswordBibleStudies.com

Psalm 91

Psalm 95

Across

2. the _____ of the hills is his also (95:4)
4. make a joyful noise unto him with _____ (95:2)
5. In his hand are the _____ places of the earth (95:4)
6. To day if ye will hear his _____ (95:7)
8. before the LORD our _____ (95:6)
10. Harden not your _____ (95:8)
14. as in the day of temptation in the _____ (95:8)
16. his _____ formed the dry land (95:5)
17. O come, let us _____ unto the LORD (95:1)
19. For the LORD is a _____ God (95:3)
20. It is a people that do err in their heart, and they have not _____ my ways (95:10)
22. that they should not enter into my _____ (95:11)
23. _____ years long was I grieved (95:10)
24. let us make a _____ noise (95:1)
25. When your fathers tempted me, proved me, and saw my _____ (95:9)

Down

1. Let us come before his _____ with thanksgiving (95:2)
3. For he is our _____ (95:7)
4. we are the _____ of his pasture (95:7)
7. O _____, let us worship (95:6)
9. let us _____ before the LORD (95:6)
10. _____ not your heart, as in the provocation (95:8)
11. let us _____ and bow down (95:6)
12. a great God, and a great _____ above all gods (95:3)
13. I grieved with this _____ (95:10)
15. the people of his pasture, and the _____ of his hand (95:7)
18. The sea is his, and he _____ it (95:5)
21. Unto whom I sware in my _____ (95:11)
22. to the _____ of our salvation (95:1)

All Clues are taken directly from the 1611 edition of the King James Version (KJV).
Crossword Bible Studies: Top 40 Classic Songs in Psalms (KJV) © 2017 Christy Bower
These puzzles are reproducible if you purchased the book.
www.CrosswordBibleStudies.com

Psalm 95

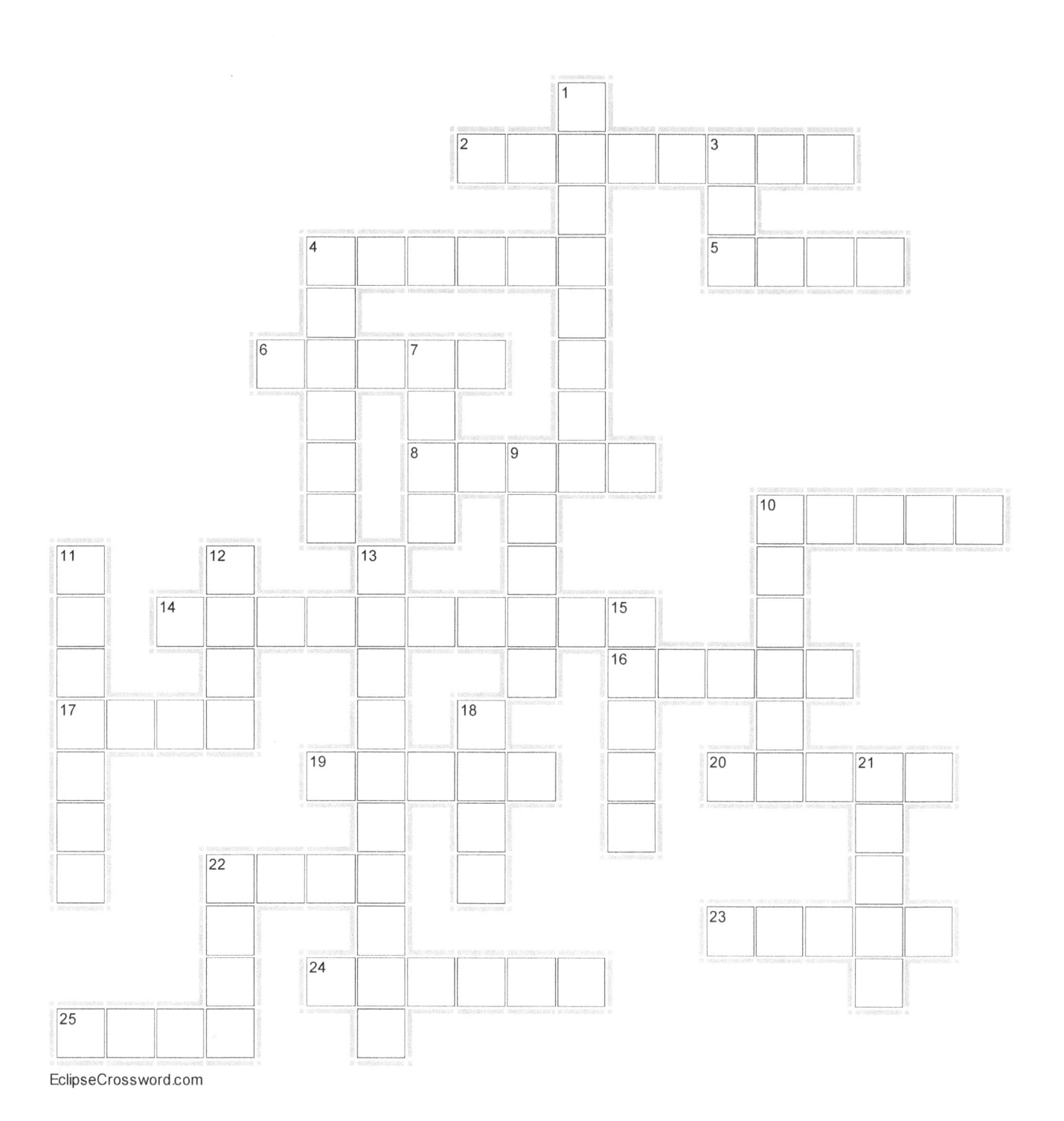

Psalm 96

Across

1. sing unto the LORD, all the _____ (96:1)
3. Say among the heathen that the _____ reigneth (96:10)
4. Sing unto the LORD, _____ his name (96:2)
7. bring an _____, and come into his courts (96:8)
8. he shall judge the world with _____, and the people with his truth (96:13)
10. Give unto the LORD the glory due unto his _____ (96:8)
11. Let the field be _____, and all that is therein: then shall all the trees of the wood rejoice (96:12)
13. give unto the LORD _____ and strength (96:7)
15. O _____ the LORD (96:9)
16. let the earth be _____ (96:11)
19. the LORD made the _____ (96:5)
22. the world also shall be established that it shall not be _____ (96:10)
23. Before the LORD: for he cometh, for he cometh to _____ the earth (96:13)
24. _____ his glory among the heathen (96:3)
25. let the _____ roar, and the fulness thereof (96:11)

Down

2. in the beauty of _____ (96:9)
5. O sing unto the LORD a new _____ (96:1)
6. _____ unto the LORD, O ye kindreds of the people (96:7)
8. Let the heavens _____ (96:11)
9. shew forth his _____ from day to day (96:2)
12. he is to be _____ above all gods (96:4)
14. For the LORD is great, and greatly to be _____ (96:4)
17. his _____ among all people (96:3)
18. Honour and _____ are before him: strength and beauty are in his sanctuary (96:6)
20. O _____ unto the LORD (96:1)
21. For all the gods of the nations are _____ (96:5)

All Clues are taken directly from the 1611 edition of the King James Version (KJV).
Crossword Bible Studies: Top 40 Classic Songs in Psalms (KJV) © 2017 Christy Bower
These puzzles are reproducible if you purchased the book.
www.CrosswordBibleStudies.com

Psalm 96

Psalm 100

Across

1. his truth endureth to all _____ (100:5)
3. _____ into his gates (100:4)
6. Enter into his gates with _____ (100:4)
9. and into his _____ with praise (100:4)
10. we are his _____ (100:3)
11. a joyful _____ unto the LORD (100:1)
12. his _____ is everlasting (100:5)
13. _____ his name (100:4)
17. Enter into his _____ (100:4)
19. the sheep of his _____ (100:3)
20. Serve the LORD with _____ (100:2)
22. made us, and not we _____ (100:3)
23. _____ a joyful noise (100:1)
24. into his courts with _____ (100:4)

Down

2. his mercy is _____ (100:5)
4. and his _____ endureth (100:5)
5. Know ye that the _____ he is God (100:3)
7. _____ ye that the LORD he is God (100:3)
8. For the LORD is _____ (100:5)
10. come before his _____ (100:2)
12. it is he that hath _____ us (100:3)
14. before his presence with _____ (100:2)
15. be _____ unto him (100:4)
16. unto the LORD, all ye _____ (100:1)
18. _____ the LORD (100:2)
21. and the _____ of his pasture (100:3)

All Clues are taken directly from the 1611 edition of the King James Version (KJV).
Crossword Bible Studies: Top 40 Classic Songs in Psalms (KJV) © 2017 Christy Bower
These puzzles are reproducible if you purchased the book.
www.CrosswordBibleStudies.com

Psalm 100

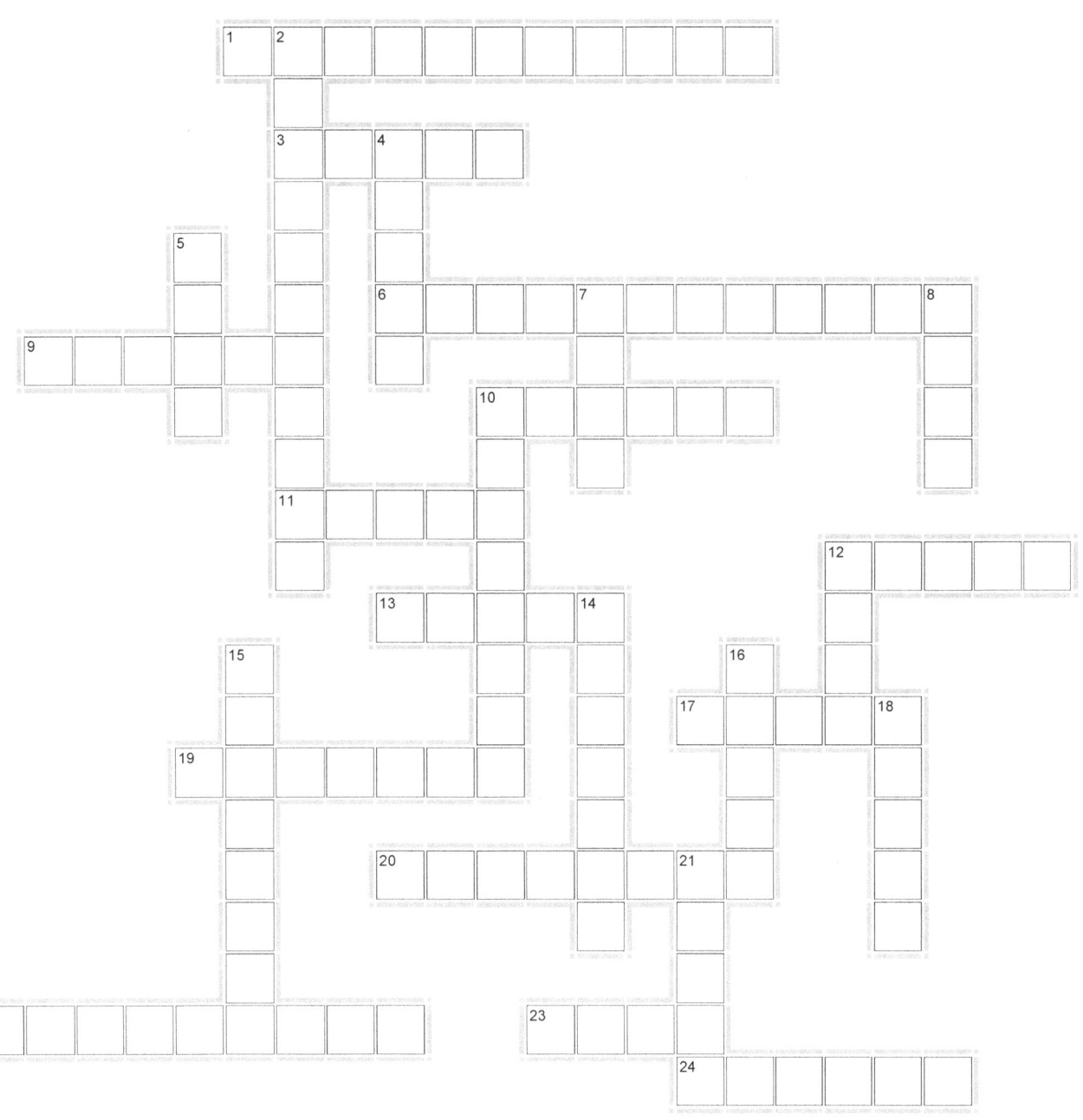

Psalm 103

Across

1. Bless the LORD, O my soul, and forget not all his _____ (103:2)
6. slow to _____, and plenteous in mercy (103:8)
8. judgment for all that are _____ (103:6)
9. But the _____ of the LORD is from everlasting to everlasting upon them that fear him (103:17)
11. He made known his ways unto _____ (103:7)
14. He hath not dealt with us after our _____; nor rewarded us according to our iniquities (103:10)
15. and his _____ unto children's children (103:17)
16. For as the heaven is high above the earth, so _____ is his mercy toward them that fear him (103:11)
18. his acts unto the children of _____ (103:7)
20. _____ ye the LORD, all ye his hosts; ye ministers of his, that do his pleasure (103:21)
21. all that is within me, bless his holy _____ (103:1)
22. For he knoweth our frame; he remembereth that we are _____ (103:14)
27. For the _____ passeth over it, and it is gone; and the place thereof shall know it no more (103:16)
28. Who redeemeth thy life from _____ (103:4)
29. his _____ ruleth over all (103:19)
31. as a _____ of the field, so he flourisheth (103:15)
32. Who forgiveth all thine _____ (103:3)
33. Like as a father pitieth his _____, so the LORD pitieth them that fear him (103:13)

Down

2. The LORD hath prepared his _____ in the heavens (103:19)
3. As for man, his days are as _____ (103:15)
4. bless the _____, O my soul (103:22)
5. that do his commandments, hearkening unto the voice of his _____ (103:20)
7. The LORD is merciful and _____ (103:8)
10. who crowneth thee with _____ and tender mercies (103:4)
12. so that thy _____ is renewed like the eagle's (103:5)
13. who healeth all thy _____ (103:3)
17. Bless the LORD, ye his _____, that excel in strength (103:20)
19. As far as the east is from the west, so far hath he _____ our transgressions from us (103:12)
23. Bless the LORD, all his works in all places of his _____ (103:22)
24. The LORD executeth righteousness and _____ (103:6)
25. Bless the LORD, O my _____ (103:1)
26. To such as keep his covenant, and to those that _____ his commandments to do them (103:18)
30. Who satisfieth thy _____ with good things (103:5)

All Clues are taken directly from the 1611 edition of the King James Version (KJV).
Crossword Bible Studies: Top 40 Classic Songs in Psalms (KJV) © 2017 Christy Bower
These puzzles are reproducible if you purchased the book.
www.CrosswordBibleStudies.com

Psalm 103

Psalm 107

Across

3. For he hath _____ the gates of brass, and cut the bars of iron in sunder (107:16)
5. Such as sit in _____ and in the shadow of death, being bound in affliction and iron (107:10)
8. Their soul abhorreth all manner of meat; and they draw near unto the gates of _____ (107:18)
11. He maketh the storm a calm, so that the waves thereof are _____ (107:29)
12. Let the _____ of the Lord say so, whom he hath redeemed from the hand of the enemy (107:2)
14. For he satisfieth the longing soul, and filleth the hungry _____ with goodness (107:9)
17. Yet setteth he the _____ on high from affliction, and maketh him families like a flock (107:41)
20. Oh that men would praise the Lord for his goodness, and for his wonderful works to the _____ of men! (107:31)
21. He blesseth them also, so that they are _____ greatly; and suffereth not their cattle to decrease (107:38)
22. these see the works of the Lord, and his _____ in the deep (107:24)
25. And there he maketh the _____ to dwell, that they may prepare a city for habitation (107:36)
26. O give _____ unto the Lord, for he is good: for his mercy endureth for ever (107:1)
28. Then they _____ unto the Lord in their trouble, and he saved them out of their distresses (107:13)
31. Then they cried unto the Lord in their trouble, and he _____ them out of their distresses (107:6)
32. He sent his word, and _____ them, and delivered them from their destructions (107:20)
33. They reel to and fro, and _____ like a drunken man, and are at their wits' end (107:27)
34. Then they cry unto the Lord in their _____, and he saveth them out of their distresses (107:19)
37. Oh that men would _____ the Lord for his goodness, and for his wonderful works to the children of men! (107:15)
38. Again, they are minished and brought low through _____, affliction, and sorrow (107:39)
39. He turneth _____ into a wilderness, and the watersprings into dry ground (107:33)

Down

1. Oh that men would praise the Lord for his goodness, and for his _____ works to the children of men! (107:21)
2. He poureth contempt upon _____, and causeth them to wander in the wilderness (107:40)
4. The _____ shall see it, and rejoice: and all iniquity shall stop her mouth (107:42)
6. and _____ them out of the lands, from the east, and from the west, from the north, and from the south (107:3)
7. He turneth the _____ into a standing water, and dry ground into watersprings (107:35)
9. And let them sacrifice the sacrifices of _____, and declare his works with rejoicing (107:22)
10. They _____ in the wilderness in a solitary way; they found no city to dwell in (107:4)
13. Fools because of their transgression, and because of their iniquities, are _____ (107:17)
14. He brought them out of darkness and the _____ of death, and brake their bands in sunder (107:14)
15. Oh that men would praise the Lord for his _____, and for his wonderful works to the children of men! (107:8)
16. They that go down to the sea in _____, that do business in great waters (107:23)
18. Whoso is _____, and will observe these things, even they shall understand the lovingkindness of the Lord (107:43)
19. Then are they _____ because they be quiet; so he bringeth them unto their desired haven (107:30)
21. their soul is _____ because of trouble (107:26)
23. they _____ against the words of God (107:11)
24. For he commandeth, and raiseth the stormy _____, which lifteth up the waves thereof (107:25)
26. Hungry and _____, their soul fainted (107:5)
27. a fruitful land into barrenness, for the _____ of them that dwell therein (107:34)
29. Let them _____ him also in the congregation of the people, and praise him in the assembly of the elders (107:32)
30. and sow the fields, and plant _____, which may yield fruits of increase (107:37)
32. he brought down their heart with labour; they fell down, and there was none to _____ (107:12)
35. Then they _____ unto the Lord in their trouble, and he bringeth them out of their distresses (107:28)
36. And he led them forth by the right way, that they might go to a _____ of habitation (107:7)

All Clues are taken directly from the 1611 edition of the King James Version (KJV).
Crossword Bible Studies: Top 40 Classic Songs in Psalms (KJV) © 2017 Christy Bower
These puzzles are reproducible if you purchased the book.
www.CrosswordBibleStudies.com

Psalm 107

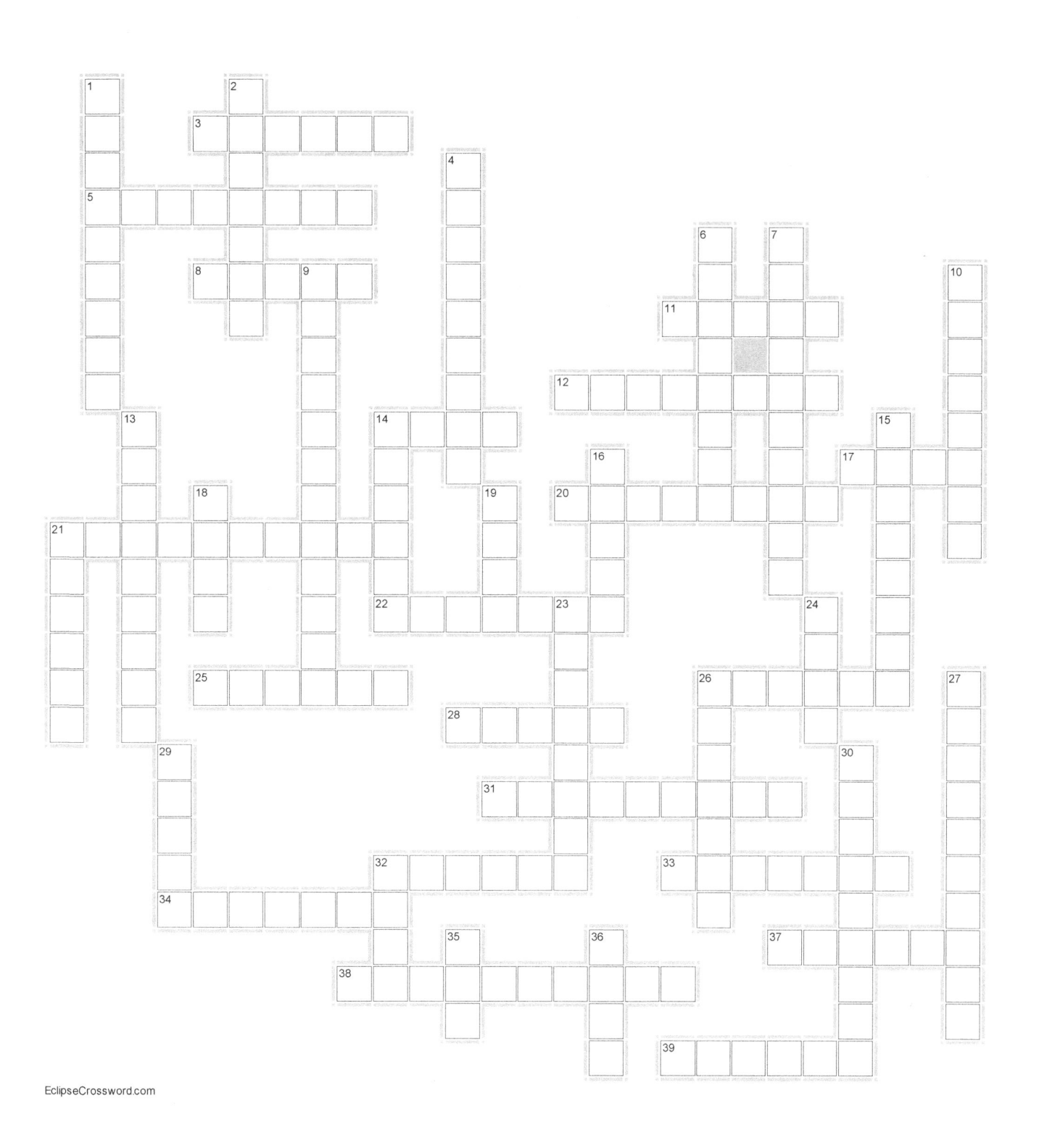

Psalm 112

Across

3. The wicked shall see it, and be _____ (112:10)
5. A _____ man sheweth favour, and lendeth (112:5)
7. he shall not be _____ (112:8)
10. His heart is _____ (112:8)
11. he will _____ his affairs with discretion (112:5)
13. that feareth the LORD, that delighteth greatly in his _____ (112:1)
15. his heart is fixed, _____ in the LORD (112:7)
16. his _____ is fixed (112:7)
19. He hath dispersed, he hath given to the _____; his righteousness endureth for ever (112:9)
21. the righteous shall be in everlasting _____ (112:6)
22. His seed shall be _____ upon earth (112:2)
23. the desire of the wicked shall _____ (112:10)
24. Unto the _____ there ariseth light (112:4)

Down

1. full of _____, and righteous (112:4)
2. _____ is the man that feareth the LORD (112:1)
4. his righteousness endureth for ever; his horn shall be _____ with honour (112:9)
6. Surely he shall not be _____ for ever (112:6)
8. there ariseth light in the _____ (112:4)
9. he shall gnash with his _____, and melt away (112:10)
11. the _____ of the upright shall be blessed (112:2)
12. until he see his desire upon his _____ (112:8)
14. his _____ endureth for ever (112:3)
17. _____ ye the LORD (112:1)
18. he is _____, and full of compassion (112:4)
20. _____ and riches shall be in his house (112:3)

All Clues are taken directly from the 1611 edition of the King James Version (KJV).
Crossword Bible Studies: Top 40 Classic Songs in Psalms (KJV) © 2017 Christy Bower
These puzzles are reproducible if you purchased the book.
www.CrosswordBibleStudies.com

Psalm 112

Psalm 115

Across

3. for thy _____, and for thy truth's sake (115:1)
4. unto thy name give _____ (115:1)
7. O _____, trust thou in the Lord (115:9)
10. should the heathen say, _____ is now their God? (115:2)
12. they have _____, but they hear not (115:6)
14. O house of _____, trust in the Lord (115:10)
15. _____ have they, but they see not (115:5)
17. They that _____ them are like unto them; so is every one that trusteth in them (115:8)
18. The dead praise not the Lord, neither any that go down into _____ (115:17)
19. neither speak they through their _____ (115:7)
20. _____ the Lord (115:18)
21. They have _____, but they speak not (115:5)
23. not unto us, but unto thy _____ give glory (115:1)
27. he will bless the _____ of Israel; he will bless the house of Aaron (115:12)
28. The Lord shall increase you more and more, you and your _____ (115:14)
29. Ye are _____ of the Lord (115:15)
32. He will bless them that fear the Lord, both _____ and great (115:13)
33. he is their _____ and their shield (115:10)
34. The _____ praise not the Lord (115:17)
35. he hath done whatsoever he hath _____ (115:3)

Down

1. Their idols are silver and gold, the _____ of men's hands (115:4)
2. But our God is in the _____ (115:3)
4. The heaven, even the heavens, are the Lord's: but the earth hath he _____ to the children of men (115:16)
5. the Lord which made heaven and _____ (115:15)
6. he will _____ us; he will bless the house of Israel (115:12)
8. Their idols are _____ and gold (115:4)
9. Ye that _____ the Lord, trust in the Lord (115:11)
11. Ye that fear the Lord, _____ in the Lord: he is their help and their shield (115:11)
13. Wherefore should the _____ say (115:2)
16. The Lord shall _____ you more and more (115:14)
19. But we will bless the Lord from this _____ forth and for evermore (115:18)
22. they have _____, but they handle not (115:7)
24. The Lord hath been _____ of us: he will bless us (115:12)
25. Not unto us, O _____, not unto us (115:1)
26. feet have they, but they _____ not (115:7)
30. he is their help and their _____ (115:9)
31. noses have they, but they _____ not (115:6)

All Clues are taken directly from the 1611 edition of the King James Version (KJV).
Crossword Bible Studies: Top 40 Classic Songs in Psalms (KJV) © 2017 Christy Bower
These puzzles are reproducible if you purchased the book.
www.CrosswordBibleStudies.com

Psalm 115

Psalm 118

Across

2. The _____ which the builders refused is become the head stone of the corner (118:22)
7. Let the house of _____ now say, that his mercy endureth for ever (118:3)
9. we will _____ and be glad in it (118:24)
11. in the name of the _____ will I destroy them (118:10)
13. the _____ hand of the Lord doeth valiantly (118:15)
17. The Lord is my _____ and song, and is become my salvation (118:14)
18. God is the Lord, which hath shewed us _____: bind the sacrifice with cords, even unto the horns of the altar (118:27)
21. O give _____ unto the Lord; for he is good: for his mercy endureth for ever (118:29)
22. _____ be he that cometh in the name of the Lord: we have blessed you out of the house of the Lord (118:26)
24. This is the day which the Lord hath _____ (118:24)
28. All _____ compassed me about (118:10)
31. for in the name of the Lord I will _____ them (118:12)
32. The voice of _____ and salvation is in the tabernacles of the righteous (118:15)
33. thou art my God, I will _____ thee (118:28)
34. I will praise thee: for thou hast heard me, and art become my _____ (118:21)
36. They compassed me about like _____ (118:12)

Down

1. Let _____ now say, that his mercy endureth for ever (118:2)
3. The right hand of the Lord is _____: the right hand of the Lord doeth valiantly (118:16)
4. O give thanks unto the Lord; for he is _____: for his mercy endureth for ever (118:29)
5. the Lord _____ me, and set me in a large place (118:5)
6. Let them now that _____ the Lord say, that his mercy endureth for ever (118:4)
8. It is better to _____ in the Lord than to put confidence in princes (118:9)
10. The Lord hath chastened me sore: but he hath not given me over unto _____ (118:18)
12. this gate of the Lord, into which the _____ shall enter (118:20)
14. Thou hast thrust sore at me that I might fall: but the Lord _____ me (118:13)
15. Open to me the _____ of righteousness: I will go into them, and I will praise the Lord (118:19)
16. Thou art my God, and I will _____ thee (118:28)
19. The Lord taketh my part with them that _____ me: therefore shall I see my desire upon them that hate me (118:7)
20. The Lord is on my side; I will not fear: what can _____ do unto me? (118:6)
23. This is the Lord's _____; it is marvellous in our eyes (118:23)
25. It is better to trust in the Lord than to put _____ in man (118:8)
26. Save now, I beseech thee, O Lord: O Lord, I beseech thee, send now _____ (118:25)
27. I called upon the Lord in _____ (118:5)
29. because his _____ endureth for ever (118:1)
30. O _____ thanks unto the Lord; for he is good (118:1)
31. I shall not die, but live, and _____ the works of the Lord (118:17)
35. They compassed me about; yea, they compassed me about: but in the _____ of the Lord I will destroy them (118:11)

All Clues are taken directly from the 1611 edition of the King James Version (KJV).
Crossword Bible Studies: Top 40 Classic Songs in Psalms (KJV) © 2017 Christy Bower
These puzzles are reproducible if you purchased the book.
www.CrosswordBibleStudies.com

Psalm 118

Psalm 119

Across

5. And I will walk at _____: for I seek thy precepts (119:45)
8. Thy word is a _____ unto my feet, and a light unto my path (119:105)
10. Thy testimonies have I taken as an _____ for ever: for they are the rejoicing of my heart (119:111)
13. Deal with thy servant according unto thy mercy, and teach me thy _____ (119:124)
14. Make me to _____ the way of thy precepts: so shall I talk of thy wondrous works (119:27)
15. _____ my voice according unto thy lovingkindness: O LORD, quicken me according to thy judgment (119:149)
16. Look thou upon me, and be _____ unto me, as thou usest to do unto those that love thy name (119:132)
18. Open thou mine eyes, that I may behold _____ things out of thy law (119:18)
21. _____ are they that keep his testimonies, and that seek him with the whole heart (119:2)
22. Princes have persecuted me without a cause: but my heart standeth in _____ of thy word (119:161)
25. Let thy tender mercies come unto me, that I may live: for thy _____ is my delight (119:77)
27. It is good for me that I have been _____; that I might learn thy statutes (119:71)
28. Consider mine affliction, and deliver me: for I do not _____ thy law (119:153)
32. I have gone astray like a lost _____; seek thy servant; for I do not forget thy commandments (119:176)
33. Let my _____ come before thee: deliver me according to thy word (119:170)
34. I cried with my _____ heart; hear me, O LORD: I will keep thy statutes (119:145)
35. I have more understanding than all my teachers: for thy _____ are my meditation (119:99)
39. Thy faithfulness is unto all _____: thou hast established the earth, and it abideth (119:90)
42. I will meditate in thy _____, and have respect unto thy ways (119:15)
44. Thy testimonies are _____: therefore doth my soul keep them (119:129)
45. How sweet are thy words unto my taste! yea, sweeter than _____ to my mouth! (119:103)
46. I am thine, _____ me; for I have sought thy precepts (119:94)
47. My _____ shall speak of thy word: for all thy commandments are righteousness (119:172)

Down

1. Thy hands have made me and _____ me: give me understanding (119:73)
2. I rejoice at thy word, as one that findeth great _____ (119:162)
3. Consider how I _____ thy precepts (119:159)
4. I remembered thy _____ of old, O LORD; and have comforted myself (119:52)
6. _____ art thou, O LORD, and upright are thy judgments (119:137)
7. Thy word have I hid in mine _____, that I might not sin against thee (119:11)
9. I will speak of thy testimonies also before kings, and will not be _____ (119:46)
11. Therefore I love thy commandments above gold; yea, above fine _____ (119:127)
12. O how love I thy law! it is my _____ all the day (119:87)
14. _____ me according unto thy word, that I may live: and let me not be ashamed (119:116)
17. Make me to go in the path of thy _____; for therein do I delight (119:35)
19. The law of thy mouth is better unto me than thousands of gold and _____ (119:72)
20. I know, O LORD, that thy judgments are right, and that thou in _____ hast afflicted me (119:75)
23. The _____, O LORD, is full of thy mercy: teach me thy statutes (119:64)
24. Unless thy law had been my delights, I should then have _____ in mine affliction (119:92)
26. Before I was afflicted I went _____: but now have I kept thy word (119:67)
29. Thy testimonies also are my _____ and my counsellors (119:24)
30. Make thy face to _____ upon thy servant; and teach me thy statutes (119:135)
31. Thou art my _____ place and my shield: I hope in thy word (119:114)
35. _____ me, O LORD, the way of thy statutes; and I shall keep it unto the end (119:33)
36. My soul fainteth for thy _____: but I hope in thy word (119:81)
37. Thy righteousness is an everlasting righteousness, and thy law is the _____ (119:142)
38. I will delight myself in thy statutes: I will not forget thy _____ (119:16)
40. Teach me good judgment and _____: for I have believed thy commandments (119:66)
41. At _____ I will rise to give thanks unto thee because of thy righteous judgments (119:62)
43. I will run the way of thy commandments, when thou shalt _____ my heart (119:32)

All Clues are taken directly from the 1611 edition of the King James Version (KJV).
Crossword Bible Studies: Top 40 Classic Songs in Psalms (KJV) © 2017 Christy Bower
These puzzles are reproducible if you purchased the book.

www.CrosswordBibleStudies.com

Psalm 119

Psalm 121

Across

3. from this _____ forth, and even for evermore (121:8)
4. shade upon thy right _____ (121:5)
5. shall not smite thee by day, nor the _____ by night (121:6)
7. he that keepeth _____ (121:4)
9. My _____ cometh from the LORD (121:2)
11. He will not suffer thy _____ to be moved (121:3)
12. I will lift up mine eyes unto the _____, from whence cometh my help (121:1)
15. heaven and _____ (121:2)
18. The LORD shall preserve thy _____ out (121:8)
19. shall preserve thee from all _____ (121:7)
20. shall neither slumber nor _____ (121:4)
21. the _____, which made heaven and earth (121:2)
23. lift up mine _____ unto the hills (121:1)

Down

1. the LORD is thy _____ upon thy right hand (121:5)
2. _____, he that keepeth Israel (121:4)
6. nor the moon by _____ (121:6)
8. thy going out and thy _____ in (121:8)
10. The LORD shall _____ thee (121:7)
13. he that keepeth thee will not _____ (121:3)
14. he shall preserve thy _____ (121:7)
16. made _____ and earth (121:2)
17. The LORD is thy _____ (121:5)
20. The _____ shall not smite thee by day (121:6)
21. I will _____ up mine eyes (121:1)
22. sun shall not smite thee by _____ (121:6)

All Clues are taken directly from the 1611 edition of the King James Version (KJV).
Crossword Bible Studies: Top 40 Classic Songs in Psalms (KJV) © 2017 Christy Bower
These puzzles are reproducible if you purchased the book.
www.CrosswordBibleStudies.com

Psalm 121

Psalm 122

Across

1. I will now say, Peace be _____ thee (122:8)
6. shall stand within thy _____, O Jerusalem (122:2)
7. the tribes of the Lord, unto the testimony of _____ (122:4)
8. a city that is _____ together (122:3)
10. the thrones of the house of _____ (122:5)
11. Jerusalem: they shall _____ that love thee (122:6)
12. Let us go into the _____ of the Lord (122:1)
15. For my _____ and companions' sakes, I will now say, Peace be within thee (122:8)
17. _____ is builded as a city that is compact (122:3)
18. _____ for the peace of Jerusalem (122:6)
20. the house of the _____ (122:1)
21. and _____ within thy palaces (122:7)
22. to give _____ unto the name of the Lord (122:4)

Down

2. unto the _____ of the Lord (122:4)
3. Jerusalem is builded as a _____ (122:3)
4. prosperity within thy _____ (122:7)
5. Because of the house of the Lord our God I will seek thy _____ (122:9)
6. I was _____ when they said unto me (122:1)
9. For there are set _____ of judgment (122:5)
11. _____ be within thy walls (122:7)
13. _____ of the house of the Lord our God (122:9)
14. Our _____ shall stand within thy gates (122:2)
16. they _____ unto me, Let us go (122:1)
19. whither the _____ go up, the tribes of the Lord (122:4)
20. they shall prosper that _____ thee (122:6)

Psalm 122

All Clues are taken directly from the 1611 edition of the King James Version (KJV).
Crossword Bible Studies: Top 40 Classic Songs in Psalms (KJV) © 2017 Christy Bower
These puzzles are reproducible if you purchased the book.
www.CrosswordBibleStudies.com

Psalm 136

Across

1. but overthrew _____ and his host in the Red sea: for his mercy endureth for ever (136:15)
5. even an heritage unto Israel his _____: for his mercy endureth for ever (136:22)
6. To him which led his people through the _____: for his mercy endureth for ever (136:16)
7. To him that _____ out the earth above the waters: for his mercy endureth for ever (136:6)
9. the moon and stars to rule by _____: for his mercy endureth for ever (136:9)
11. with a strong _____, and with a stretched out arm: for his mercy endureth for ever (136:12)
14. and brought out _____ from among them: for his mercy endureth for ever (136:11)
17. O give thanks unto the Lord; for he is _____: for his mercy endureth for ever (136:1)
18. Who _____ us in our low estate: for his mercy endureth for ever (136:23)
19. Who giveth _____ to all flesh: for his mercy endureth for ever (136:25)
20. To him that stretched out the earth above the _____: for his mercy endureth for ever (136:6)
21. To him that made great _____: for his mercy endureth for ever (136:7)
23. To him which _____ the Red sea into parts: for his mercy endureth for ever (136:13)
24. To him which smote great _____: for his mercy endureth for ever (136:17)
25. and Og the king of _____: for his mercy endureth for ever (136:20)

Down

1. and made Israel to _____ through the midst of it: for his mercy endureth for ever (136:14)
2. and hath _____ us from our enemies: for his mercy endureth for ever (136:24)
3. O give thanks unto the God of heaven: for his _____ endureth for ever (136:26)
4. To him that smote Egypt in their _____: for his mercy endureth for ever (136:10)
7. the _____ to rule by day: for his mercy endureth for ever (136:8)
8. O _____ thanks unto the Lord; for he is good: for his mercy endureth for ever (136:1)
10. O give thanks unto the God of _____: for his mercy endureth for ever (136:26)
12. Sihon king of the _____: for his mercy endureth for ever (136:19)
13. To him that by _____ made the heavens: for his mercy endureth for ever (136:5)
15. O give thanks to the _____ of lords: for his mercy endureth for ever (136:3)
16. and slew _____ kings: for his mercy endureth for ever (136:18)
17. O give thanks unto the _____ of gods: for his mercy endureth for ever (136:2)
20. To him who alone doeth great _____: for his mercy endureth for ever (136:4)
21. and gave their _____ for an heritage: for his mercy endureth for ever (136:21)
22. O give _____ unto the God of gods: for his mercy endureth for ever (136:2)

All Clues are taken directly from the 1611 edition of the King James Version (KJV).
Crossword Bible Studies: Top 40 Classic Songs in Psalms (KJV) © 2017 Christy Bower
These puzzles are reproducible if you purchased the book.
www.CrosswordBibleStudies.com

Psalm 136

Psalm 137

Across

1. O _____, let my right hand forget her cunning (137:5)
4. daughter of Babylon, who art to be _____ (137:8)
6. let my tongue cleave to the roof of my _____ (137:6)
9. they that carried us away captive _____ of us a song (137:3)
12. there we _____ down (137:1)
13. How shall we sing the Lord's _____ (137:4)
14. _____ the Lord's song (137:4)
15. If I _____ thee, O Jerusalem (137:5)
16. By the _____ of Babylon (137:1)
17. they that carried us away _____ (137:3)
21. How shall we sing the Lord's song in a _____ land? (137:4)
23. By the rivers of _____, there we sat (137:1)
24. For there they that _____ us away (137:3)
25. yea, we _____, when we remembered (137:1)
26. and they that _____ us (137:3)

Down

2. Remember, O Lord, the children of _____ in the day of Jerusalem (137:7)
3. who said, Rase it, rase it, even to the _____ thereof (137:7)
5. We hanged our harps upon the _____ in the midst thereof (137:2)
7. We hanged our _____ upon the willows in the midst thereof (137:2)
8. saying, Sing us one of the songs of _____ (137:3)
10. O _____ of Babylon (137:8)
11. they that wasted us required of us _____ (137:3)
13. rewardeth thee as thou hast _____ us (137:8)
16. we wept, when we _____ Zion (137:1)
18. let my _____ hand forget her cunning (137:5)
19. _____ shall he be, that rewardeth thee (137:8)
20. if I prefer not Jerusalem above my chief _____ (137:6)
22. If I do not remember thee, let my _____ cleave to the roof of my mouth (137:6)

All Clues are taken directly from the 1611 edition of the King James Version (KJV).
Crossword Bible Studies: Top 40 Classic Songs in Psalms (KJV) © 2017 Christy Bower
These puzzles are reproducible if you purchased the book.
www.CrosswordBibleStudies.com

Psalm 137

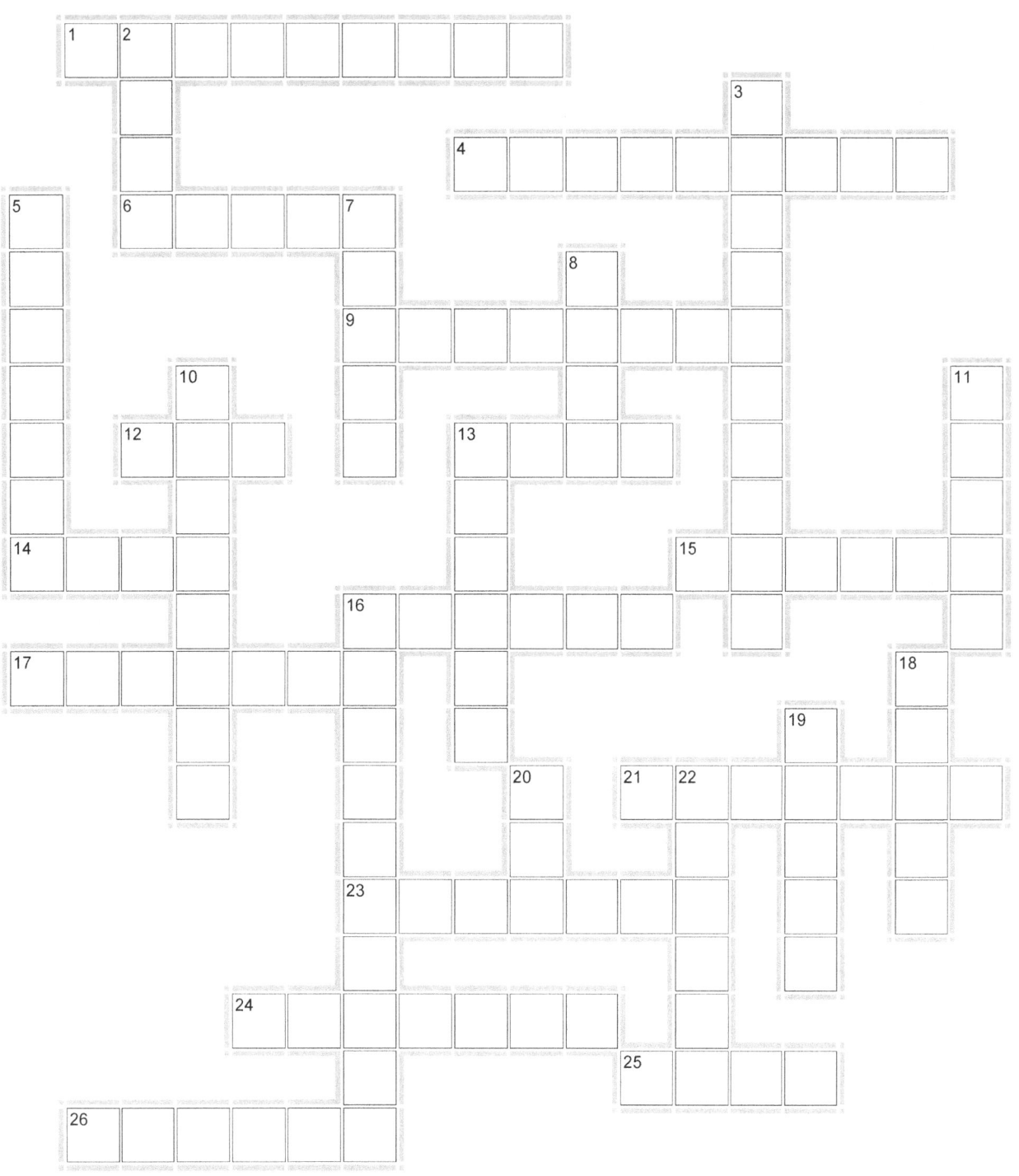

Psalm 138

Across

5. _____ not the works of thine own hands (138:8)
7. but the _____ he knoweth afar off (138:6)
9. before the _____ will I sing praise unto thee (138:1)
11. when I _____ thou answeredst me (138:3)
13. hath he respect unto the _____ (138:6)
15. praise thee with my _____ heart (138:1)
18. for thy lovingkindness and for thy _____ (138:2)
19. All the _____ of the earth shall praise thee (138:4)
21. I will _____ toward thy holy temple (138:2)
24. against the wrath of mine _____ (138:7)
26. in the midst of trouble, thou wilt _____ me (138:7)
27. thou shalt _____ forth thine hand (138:7)

Down

1. thou answeredst me, and strengthenedst me with _____ in my soul (138:3)
2. the glory of the _____ (138:5)
3. and praise thy _____ for thy lovingkindness (138:2)
4. thy _____, O Lord, endureth for ever (138:8)
6. for _____ is the glory of the Lord (138:5)
8. In the _____ when I cried thou answeredst me (138:3)
10. with strength in my _____ (138:3)
12. when they hear the words of thy _____ (138:4)
14. I will _____ thee (138:1)
16. kings of the _____ shall praise thee, O Lord (138:4)
17. for thou hast _____ thy word above all thy name (138:2)
20. Yea, they shall _____ in the ways of the Lord (138:5)
21. Though I _____ in the midst of trouble (138:7)
22. thy right hand shall _____ me (138:7)
23. The Lord will _____ that which concerneth me (138:8)
25. Though the Lord be _____, yet hath he respect unto the lowly (138:6)

All Clues are taken directly from the 1611 edition of the King James Version (KJV).
Crossword Bible Studies: Top 40 Classic Songs in Psalms (KJV) © 2017 Christy Bower
These puzzles are reproducible if you purchased the book.
www.CrosswordBibleStudies.com

Psalm 138

Psalm 139

Across

4. O LORD, thou hast _____ me, and known me (139:1)
7. How _____ also are thy thoughts unto me, O God! how great is the sum of them (139:17)
11. Thou knowest my downsitting and mine uprising, thou understandest my _____ afar off (139:2)
12. If I take the _____ of the morning (139:9)
13. Yea, the darkness hideth not from thee; but the night shineth as the day: the darkness and the _____ are both alike to thee (139:12)
15. Such knowledge is too _____ for me; it is high, I cannot attain unto it (139:6)
17. Whither shall I go from thy _____? (139:7)
21. Even there shall thy hand _____ me, and thy right hand shall hold me (139:10)
22. dwell in the uttermost parts of the _____ (139:9)
23. For they speak against thee wickedly, and thine _____ take thy name in vain (139:20)
24. know my _____ (139:23)
26. Thou compassest my path and my lying down, and art _____ with all my ways (139:3)
27. For thou hast possessed my reins: thou hast covered me in my mother's _____ (139:13)
28. If I should count them, they are more in number than the _____: when I awake, I am still with thee (139:18)

Down

1. And see if there be any wicked way in me, and lead me in the way _____ (139:24)
2. Surely thou wilt slay the _____, O God: depart from me therefore, ye bloody men (139:19)
3. _____ me, O God (139:23)
5. My substance was not hid from thee, when I was made in _____, and curiously wrought in the lowest parts of the earth (139:15)
6. Thine eyes did see my substance, yet being unperfect; and in thy _____ all my members were written, which in continuance were fashioned, when as yet there was none of them (139:16)
8. whither shall I flee from thy _____? (139:7)
9. I hate them with perfect hatred: I _____ them mine enemies (139:22)
10. if I make my bed in _____, behold, thou art there (139:8)
14. Thou hast beset me behind and before, and laid thine _____ upon me (139:5)
15. I am fearfully and _____ made (139:14)
16. Do not I hate them, O LORD, that hate thee? and am not I _____ with those that rise up against thee? (139:21)
18. I will _____ thee (139:14)
19. For there is not a word in my _____, but, lo, O LORD, thou knowest it altogether (139:4)
20. If I say, Surely the _____ shall cover me; even the night shall be light about me (139:11)
24. If I ascend up into _____, thou art there (139:8)
25. try me, and _____ my thoughts (139:23)

All Clues are taken directly from the 1611 edition of the King James Version (KJV).
Crossword Bible Studies: Top 40 Classic Songs in Psalms (KJV) © 2017 Christy Bower
These puzzles are reproducible if you purchased the book.
www.CrosswordBibleStudies.com

Psalm 139

Psalm 145

Across

5. The LORD preserveth all them that _____ him: but all the wicked will he destroy (145:20)
6. And men shall speak of the might of thy terrible acts: and I will _____ thy greatness (145:6)
8. his greatness is _____ (145:3)
10. He will fulfil the desire of them that fear him: he also will hear their cry, and will _____ them (145:19)
11. All thy works shall praise thee, O LORD; and thy _____ shall bless thee (145:10)
15. The LORD is _____, and full of compassion (145:8)
18. The LORD is nigh unto all them that call upon him, to all that call upon him in _____ (145:18)
19. They shall abundantly utter the _____ of thy great goodness (145:7)
20. They shall speak of the glory of thy _____, and talk of thy power (145:11)
23. his tender mercies are over all his _____ (145:9)
26. full of compassion; slow to _____, and of great mercy (145:8)
27. The LORD is righteous in all his ways, and _____ in all his works (145:17)
28. _____ is the LORD, and greatly to be praised (145:3)

Down

1. The LORD is good to _____ (145:9)
2. My _____ shall speak the praise of the LORD (145:21)
3. Every day will I bless thee; and I will _____ thy name for ever and ever (145:2)
4. Thy kingdom is an everlasting kingdom, and thy dominion endureth throughout all _____ (145:13)
7. I will _____ thy name for ever and ever (145:1)
9. Thy kingdom is an _____ kingdom, and thy dominion endureth throughout all generations (145:13)
12. and shall _____ of thy righteousness (145:7)
13. I will _____ thee, my God, O king (145:1)
14. Thou openest thine hand, and satisfiest the _____ of every living thing (145:16)
16. To make known to the sons of men his mighty acts, and the _____ majesty of his kingdom (145:12)
17. I will speak of the glorious honour of thy _____, and of thy wondrous works (145:5)
21. let all flesh bless his holy _____ for ever and ever (145:21)
22. One generation shall praise thy works to another, and shall declare thy _____ acts (145:4)
24. The LORD upholdeth all that _____, and raiseth up all those that be bowed down (145:14)
25. The eyes of all _____ upon thee; and thou givest them their meat in due season (145:15)

All Clues are taken directly from the 1611 edition of the King James Version (KJV).
Crossword Bible Studies: Top 40 Classic Songs in Psalms (KJV) © 2017 Christy Bower
These puzzles are reproducible if you purchased the book.
www.CrosswordBibleStudies.com

Psalm 145

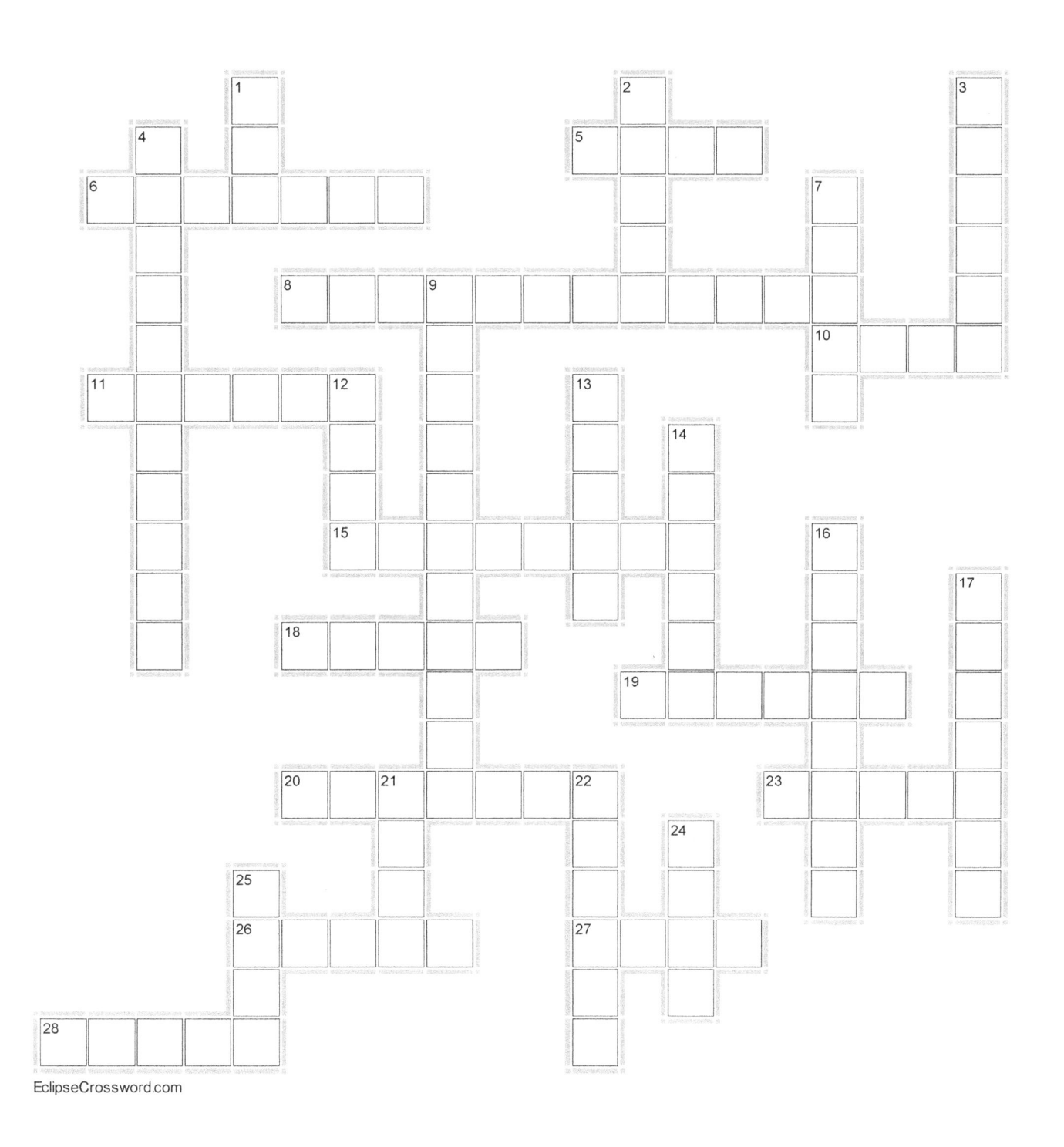

Bonus Puzzle: Book of Psalms

The bonus puzzle is an excerpt from *Crossword Bible Studies: Books of the Old Testament.*

Across

4. For thou hast been a shelter for me, and a strong _____ from the enemy (61:3)
5. Cast me not away from thy _____; and take not thy holy spirit from me (51:11)
7. Let us come before his presence with _____ (95:2)
8. So _____ us to number our days, that we may apply our hearts unto wisdom (90:12)
11. O my God, I trust in thee: let me not be ashamed, let not mine enemies _____ over me (25:2)
12. O give _____ unto the Lord; call upon his name: make known his deeds among the people (105:1)
15. O come, let us _____ and bow down (95:6)
18. _____ me from my sin (51:2)
19. For thou, Lord, art good, and ready to _____; and plenteous in mercy unto all them that call upon thee (86:5)
20. Thy _____ is a lamp unto my feet, and a light unto my path (119:105)
22. For the Lord God is a sun and _____ (84:11)
23. praise him upon the high sounding _____ (150:5)
25. The Lord is my _____ and my shield (28:7)
27. Enter into his _____ with thanksgiving (100:4)
28. _____ thy way unto the Lord; trust also in him; and he shall bring it to pass (37:5)
33. Because thy _____ is better than life, my lips shall praise thee (63:3)
35. Search me, O God, and know my _____ (139:23)
36. For the Lord is good; his mercy is _____ (100:5)
37. Create in me a clean heart, O God; and renew a right _____ within me (51:10)

Down

1. I will call upon the Lord, who is _____ to be praised: so shall I be saved from mine enemies (18:3)
2. _____ Trust in him at all times; ye people, pour out your heart before him (62:8)
3. The Lord is my rock, and my fortress, and my _____ (18:2)
6. Let the words of my mouth, and the _____ of my heart, be acceptable in thy sight (19:14)
9. O come, let us _____ unto the Lord: let us make a joyful noise to the rock of our salvation (95:1)
10. The Lord is my _____; I shall not want (23:1)
13. we are his people, and the _____ of his pasture (100:3)
14. O sing unto the Lord a new _____: sing unto the Lord, all the earth (96:1)
16. Restore unto me the joy of thy _____ (51:12)
17. Thou preparest a table before me in the presence of mine _____ (23:5)
21. But thou, O Lord, art a God full of _____, and gracious, longsuffering, and plenteous in mercy and truth (86:15)
24. With _____ and sound of cornet make a joyful noise before the Lord, the King (98:6)
26. He shall cover thee with his _____, and under his wings shalt thou trust (91:4)
29. O send out thy light and thy _____: let them lead me (43:3)
30. But I will _____ continually, and will yet praise thee more and more (71:14)
31. Why art thou cast down, O my _____? (42:5)
32. I will bless the Lord at all times: his _____ shall continually be in my mouth (34:1)
34. _____ unto God with the voice of triumph (47:1)

All Clues are taken directly from the 1611 edition of the King James Version (KJV).
Crossword Bible Studies: Top 40 Classic Songs in Psalms (KJV) © 2017 Christy Bower
These puzzles are reproducible if you purchased the book.
www.CrosswordBibleStudies.com

Bonus Puzzle: Book of Psalms

The bonus puzzle is an excerpt from *Crossword Bible Studies: Books of the Old Testament*.

All Clues are taken directly from the 1611 edition of the King James Version (KJV).
Crossword Bible Studies: Top 40 Classic Songs in Psalms (KJV) © 2017 Christy Bower
These puzzles are reproducible if you purchased the book.
www.CrosswordBibleStudies.com

Crossword Bible Studies: Books of the Old Testament

The bonus puzzle is an excerpt from *Crossword Bible Studies: Books of the Old Testament*. Featuring a crossword puzzle for each book of the Old Testament (39 puzzles), this volume provides a quick overview of the contents of the Old Testament. Whether you'd like to explore the Old Testament for the first time or review your familiarity with these books of the Bible, *Crossword Bible Studies: Books of the Old Testament* would make a good choice for your next crossword book.

Coming Soon!

Additional volumes in development:

- Women of the Bible
- Bible Heroes
- Life of David
- Genesis
- Prayers of the Bible
- Miracles of the Bible
- The Birth of Christ
- and more!

To make sure you don't miss future releases, join Christy's Friend List (one or two emails per month):

http://christybower.com/email/

All Clues are taken directly from the 1611 edition of the King James Version (KJV).
Crossword Bible Studies: Top 40 Classic Songs in Psalms (KJV) © 2017 Christy Bower
These puzzles are reproducible if you purchased the book.
www.CrosswordBibleStudies.com

Solutions

Psalm 1

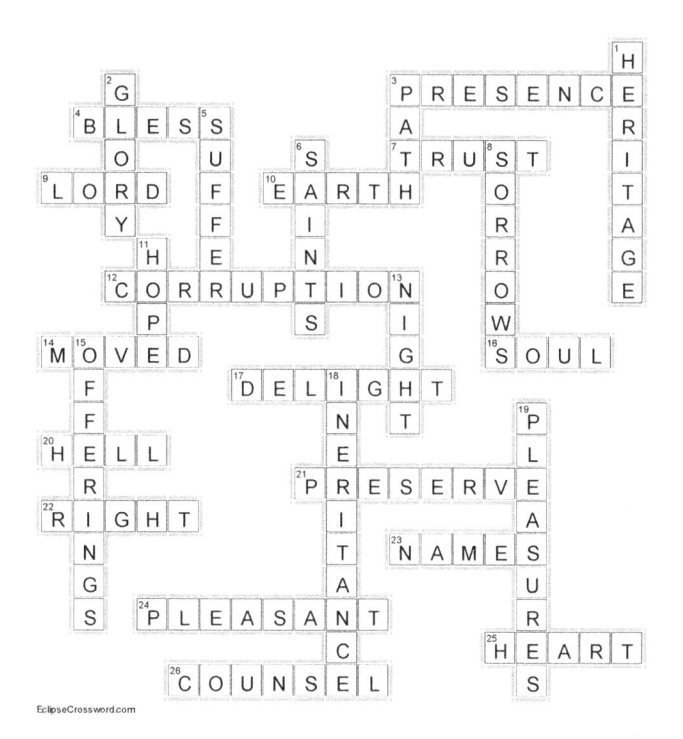

Across/Down solution grid with answers including: MEDITATE, WITHER, CHAFF, SEASON, FRUIT, PROSPER, COUNSEL, WAY, JUDGMENT, WIND, LAW, UNGODLY, NIGHT, PERISH, BLESSED, LORD, WATER, TREE, STAND, SINNERS, RIGHTEOUS.

Psalm 16

Solution grid with answers including: GLORY, BLESS, SUFFICIENT, HERITAGE, PRESENCE, TRUST, LORD, SORROW, EARTH, HEATHEN, CORRUPTION, SIGNS, MOVED, OFFERINGS, DELIGHT, SOUL, HELL, PRESERVE, PLEASURE, RIGHT, NAMES, HEART, PLEASANT, COUNSEL.

Psalm 8

Solution grid with answers including: ANGELS, CROWN, VENGEANCE, STRENGTH, EXCELLENT, NAME, MINDFUL, EARTH, SEA, LORD, HEAVEN, GLORY, STARS, OVER, ENEMY, FIGHT, MOON, CONSIDER, OUT, DOMINION, FIELD, HANDS, FISH, AIR, SHEEP, ORDAINED.

Psalm 18

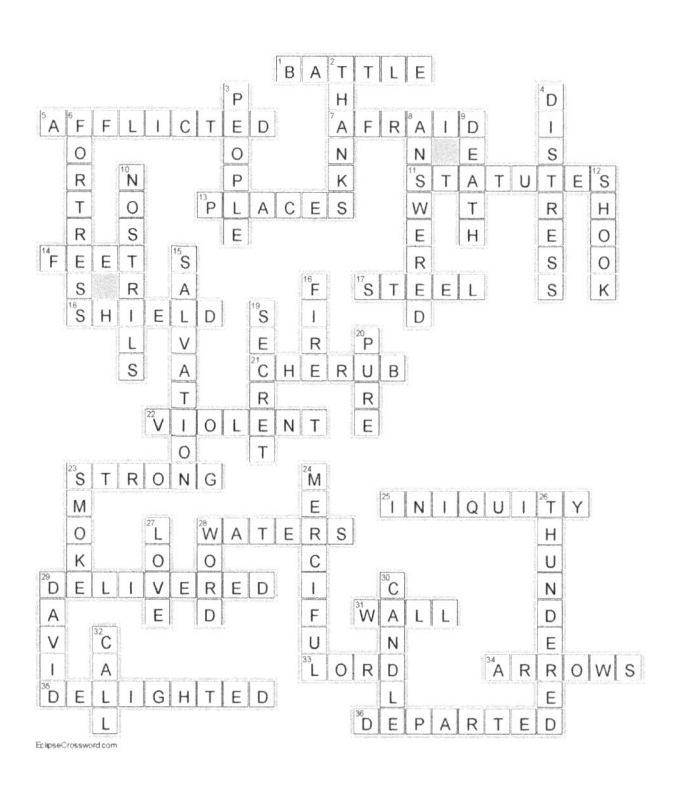

Solution grid with answers including: BATTLE, PROUD, THINE, AFRAID, DISTRESS, AFFLICTED, FORTRESS, NOSE, NECK, STATUTES, PLACES, WITH, THE, ROCK, FEET, SAVE, AIR, STEEL, HILLS, SHIELD, SEE, PREY, CHERUB, VIOLENT, STRONG, SMOKE, LIGHT, WATERS, MERCIFUL, INIQUITY, HUNDRED, DELIVERED, AVAIL, CAL, WALL, LORD, ARROWS, DELIGHTED, DEPARTED.

All Clues are taken directly from the 1611 edition of the King James Version (KJV).
Crossword Bible Studies: Top 40 Classic Songs in Psalms (KJV) © 2017 Christy Bower
These puzzles are reproducible if you purchased the book.
www.CrosswordBibleStudies.com

Psalm 19

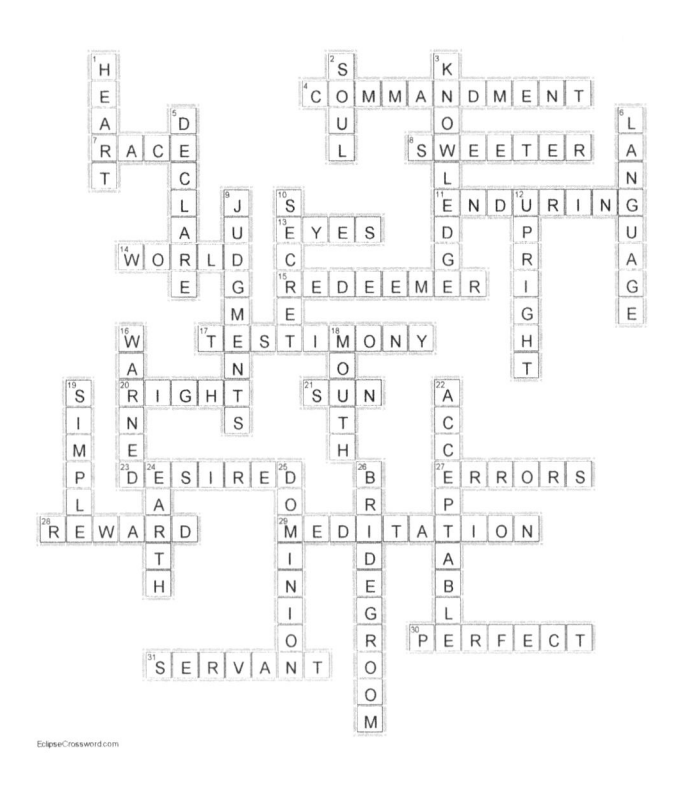

Psalm 24

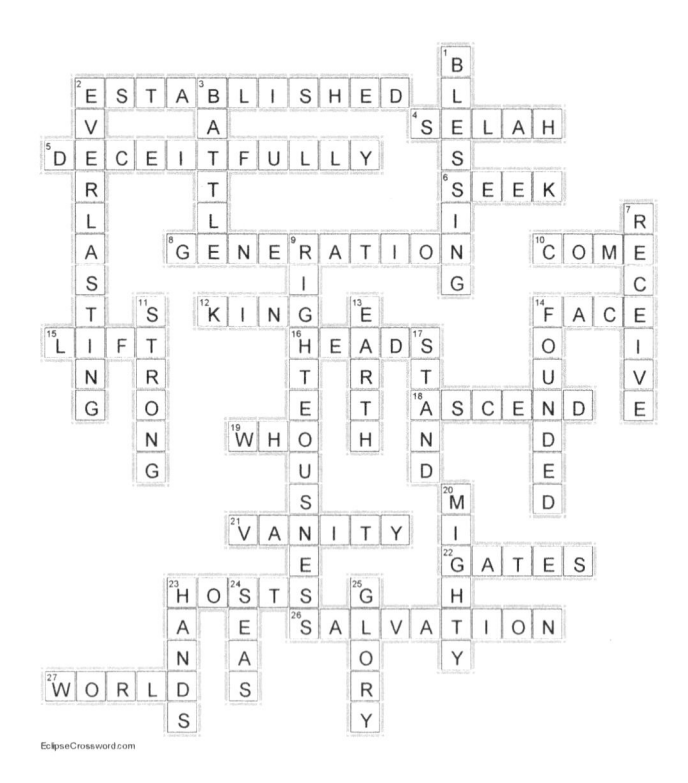

Psalm 23

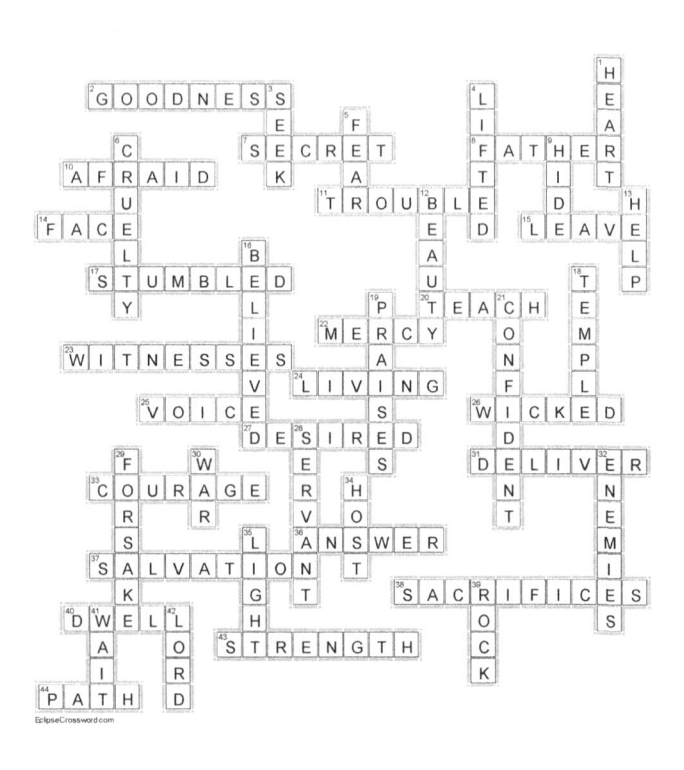

Psalm 27

All Clues are taken directly from the 1611 edition of the King James Version (KJV).
Crossword Bible Studies: Top 40 Classic Songs in Psalms (KJV) © 2017 Christy Bower
These puzzles are reproducible if you purchased the book.
www.CrosswordBibleStudies.com

Psalm 32

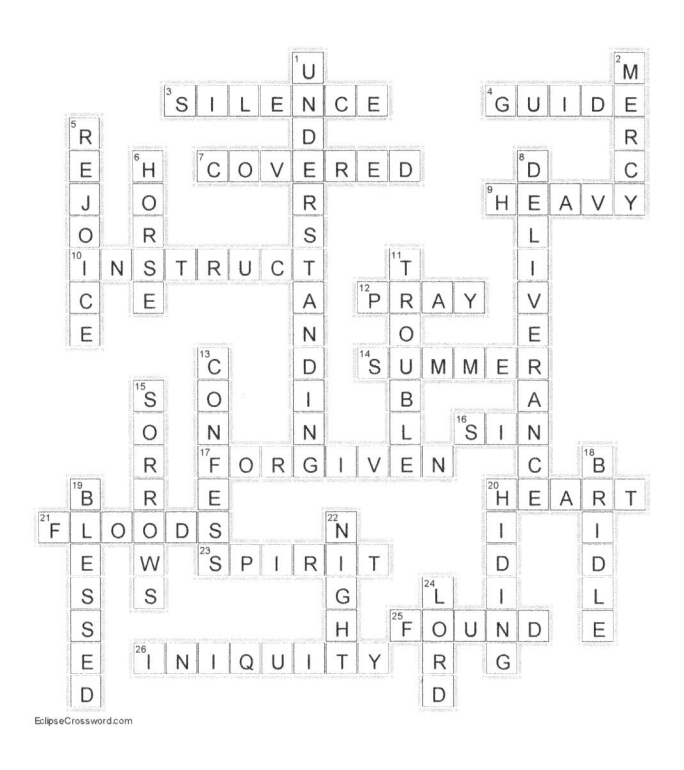

Psalm 34

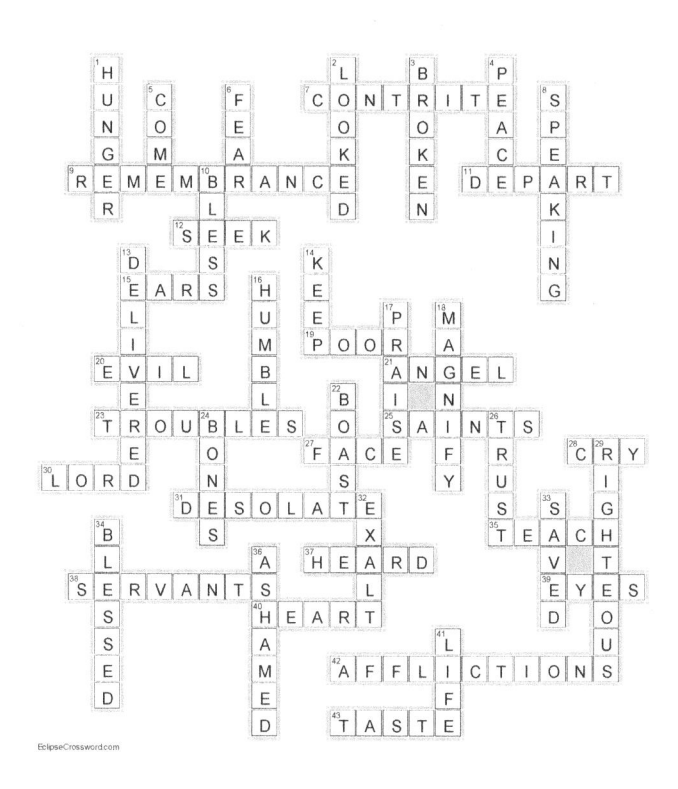

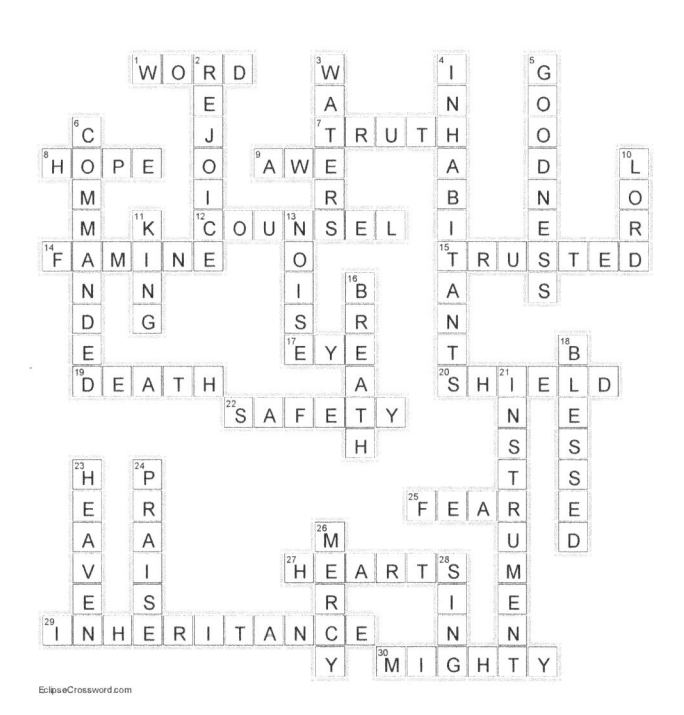

Psalm 33

Psalm 37

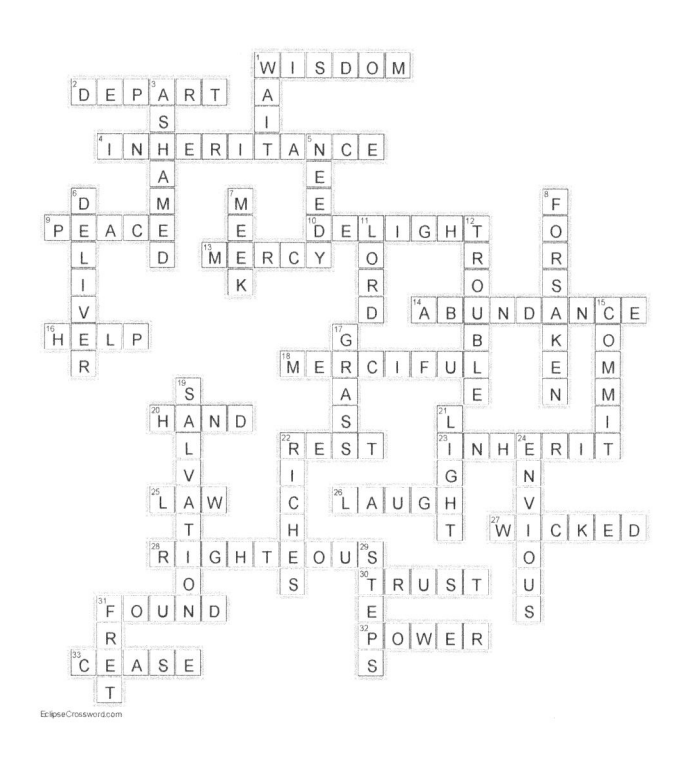

All Clues are taken directly from the 1611 edition of the King James Version (KJV).
Crossword Bible Studies: Top 40 Classic Songs in Psalms (KJV) © 2017 Christy Bower
These puzzles are reproducible if you purchased the book.
www.CrosswordBibleStudies.com

Psalm 40

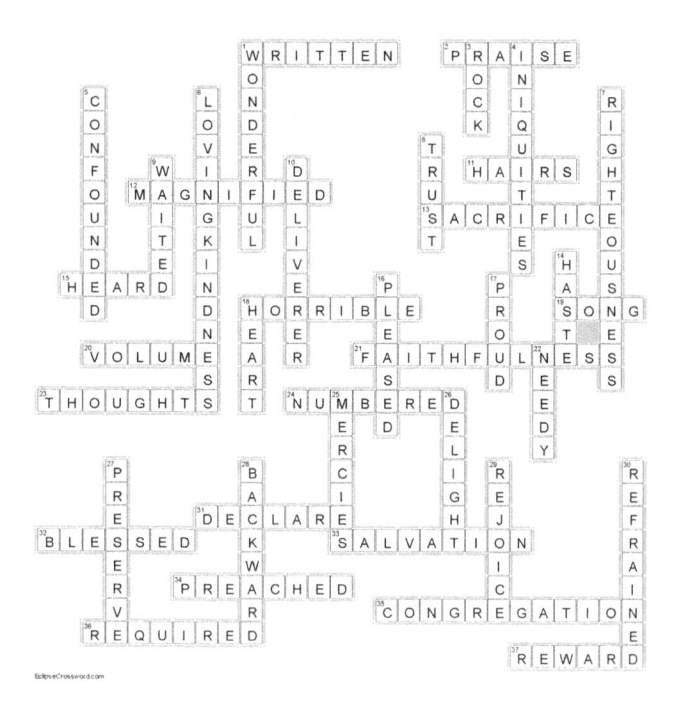

Psalm 46

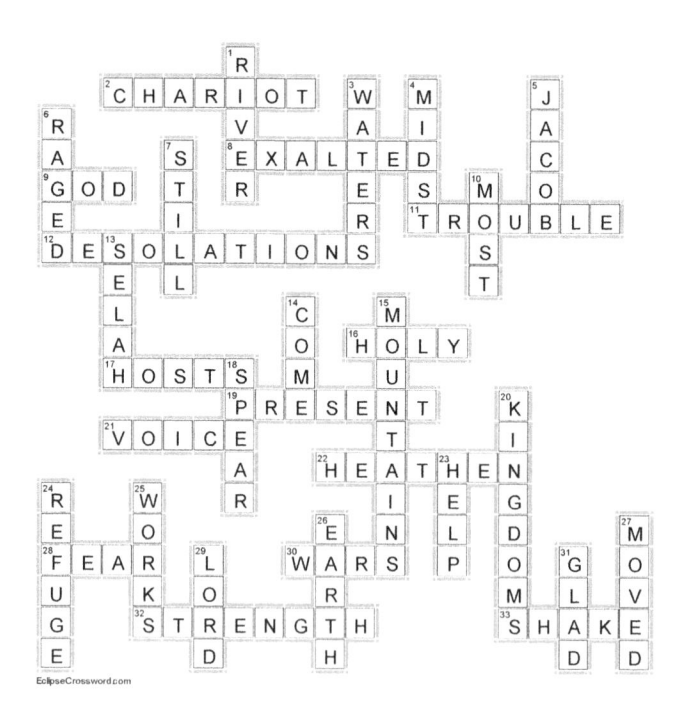

Psalm 42

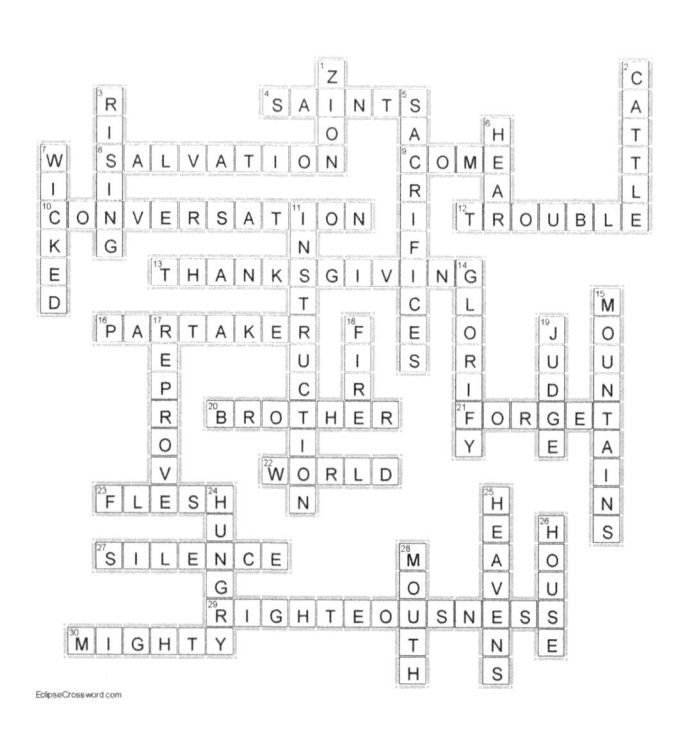

Psalm 50

All Clues are taken directly from the 1611 edition of the King James Version (KJV).
Crossword Bible Studies: Top 40 Classic Songs in Psalms (KJV) © 2017 Christy Bower
These puzzles are reproducible if you purchased the book.
www.CrosswordBibleStudies.com

Psalm 51

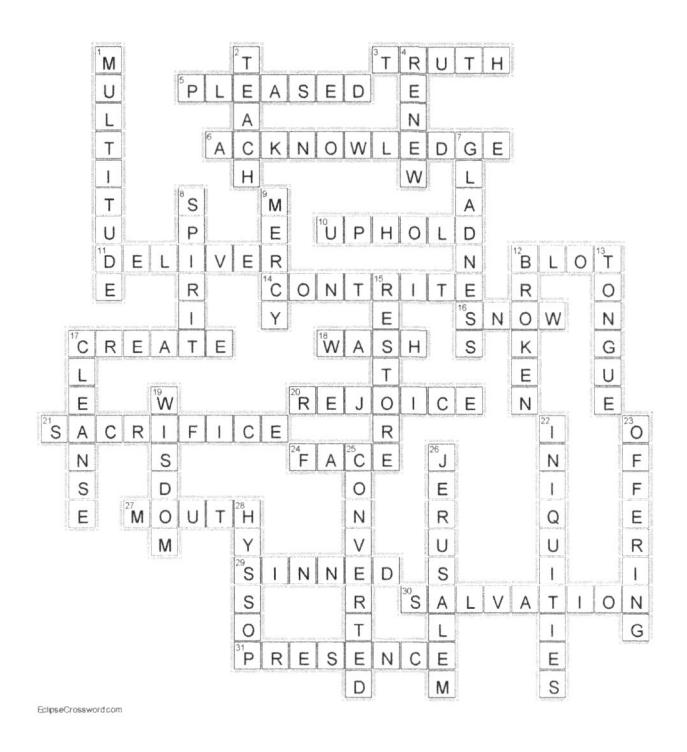

Psalm 62

Psalm 56

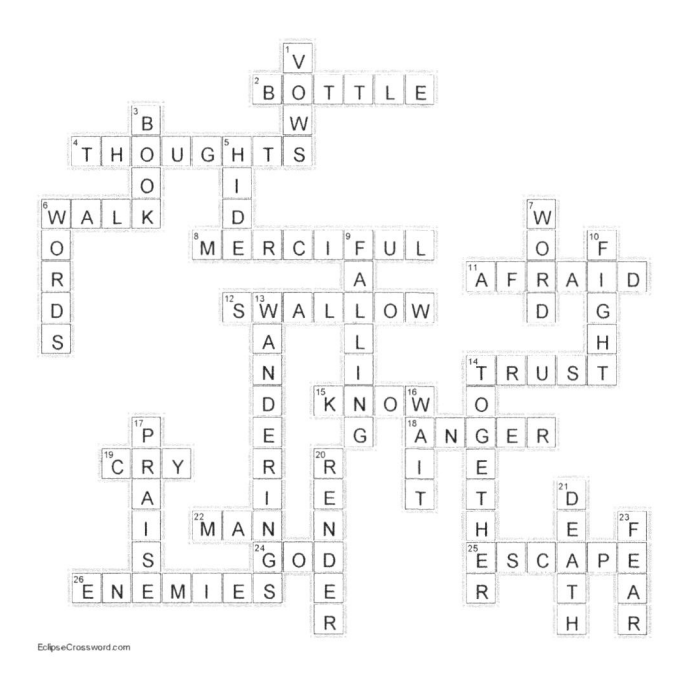

Psalm 63

All Clues are taken directly from the 1611 edition of the King James Version (KJV).
Crossword Bible Studies: Top 40 Classic Songs in Psalms (KJV) © 2017 Christy Bower
These puzzles are reproducible if you purchased the book.
www.CrosswordBibleStudies.com

Psalm 67

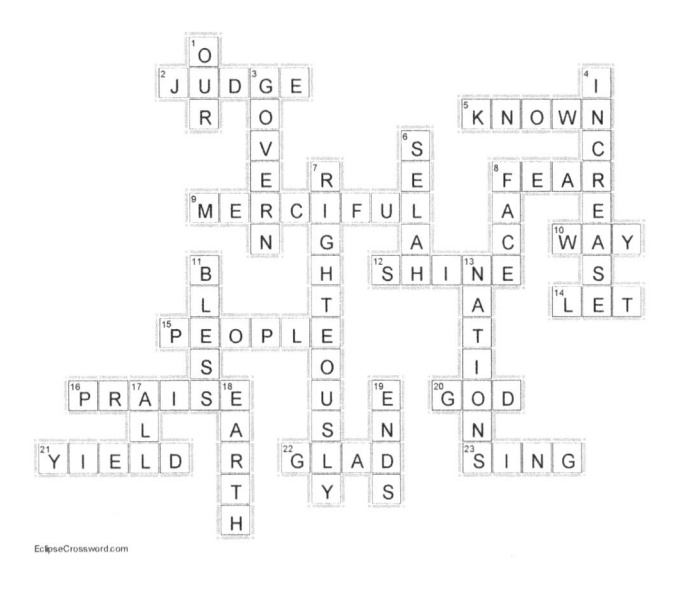

Psalm 84

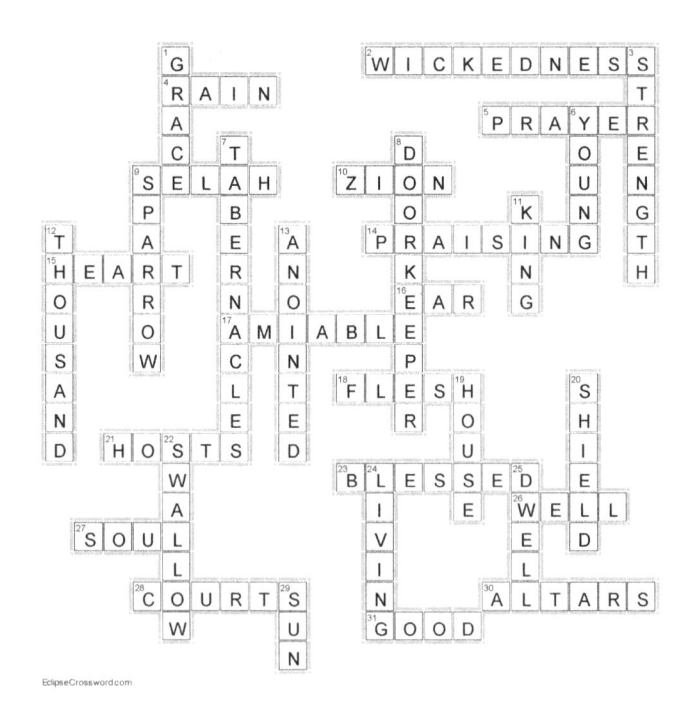

Psalm 73

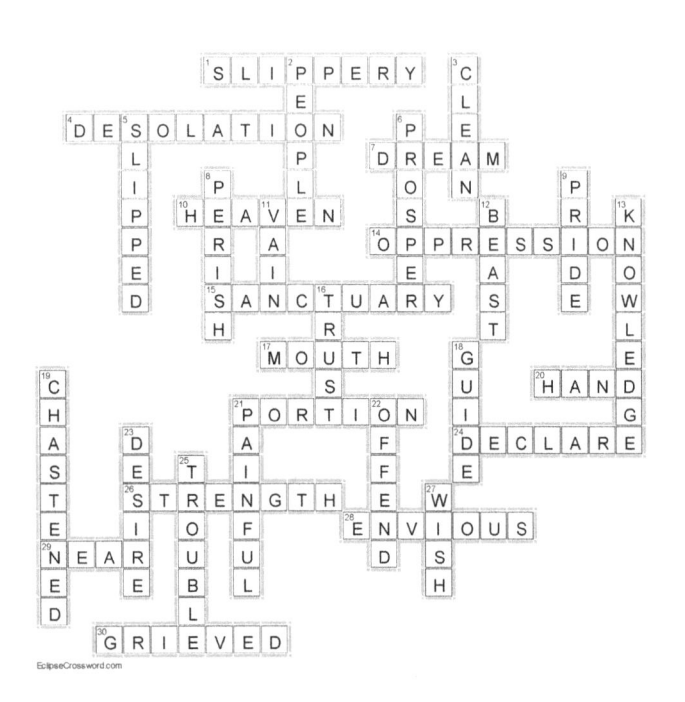

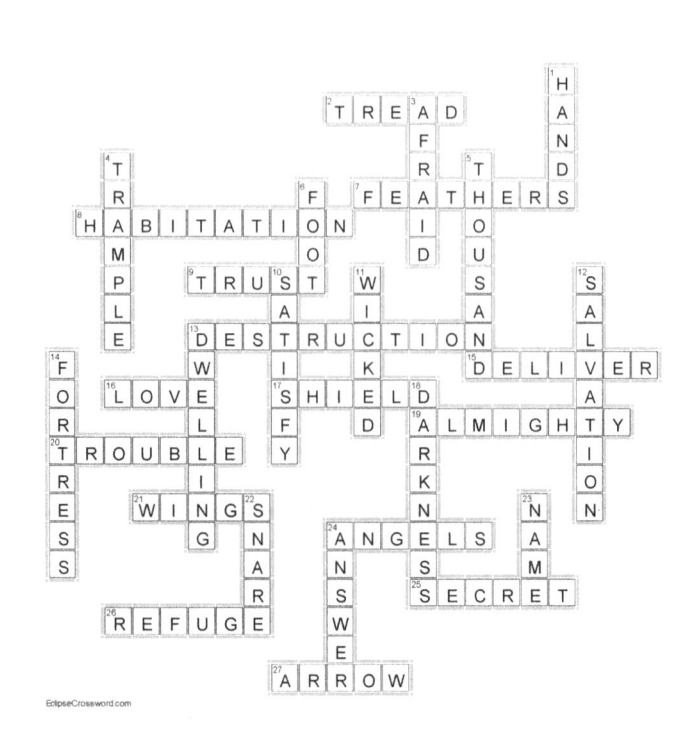

Psalm 91

All Clues are taken directly from the 1611 edition of the King James Version (KJV).
Crossword Bible Studies: Top 40 Classic Songs in Psalms (KJV) © 2017 Christy Bower
These puzzles are reproducible if you purchased the book.
www.CrosswordBibleStudies.com

Psalm 95

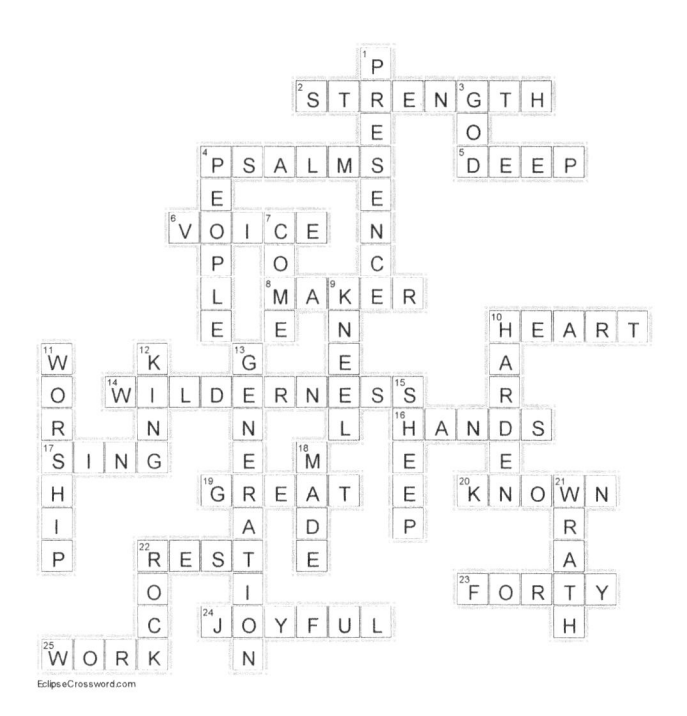

Psalm 100

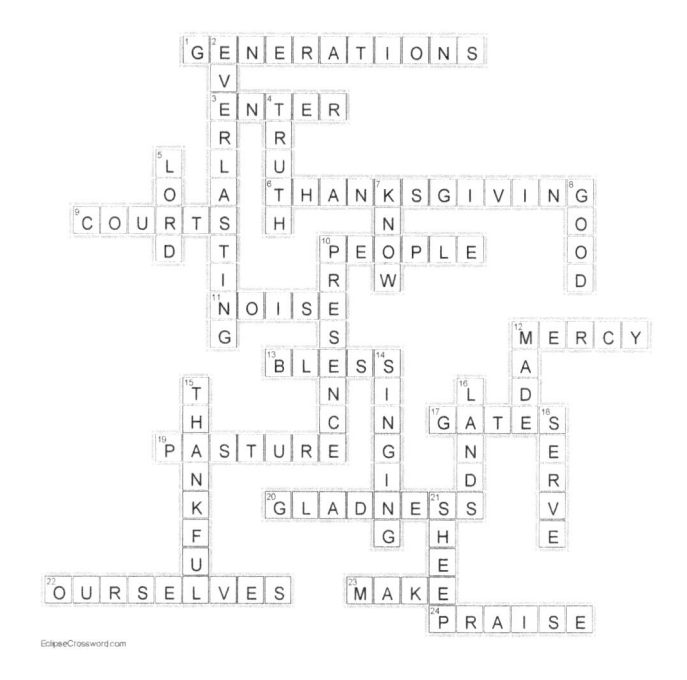

Psalm 96

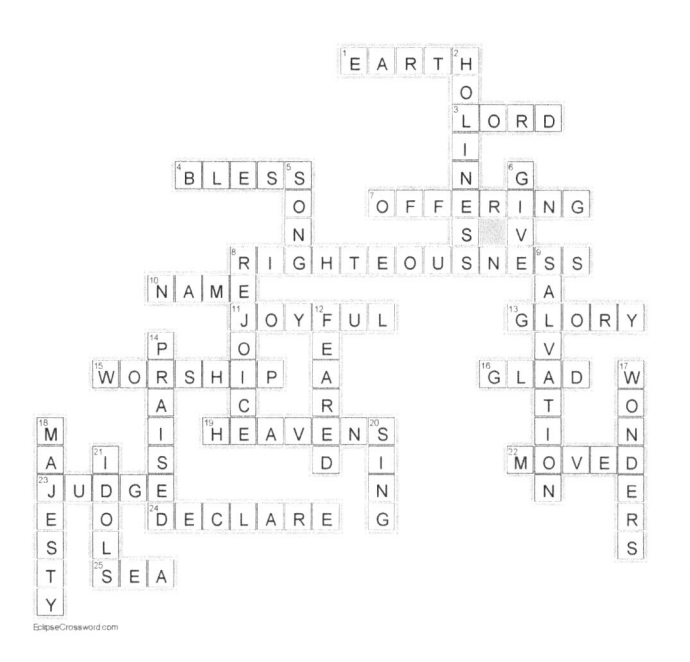

Psalm 103

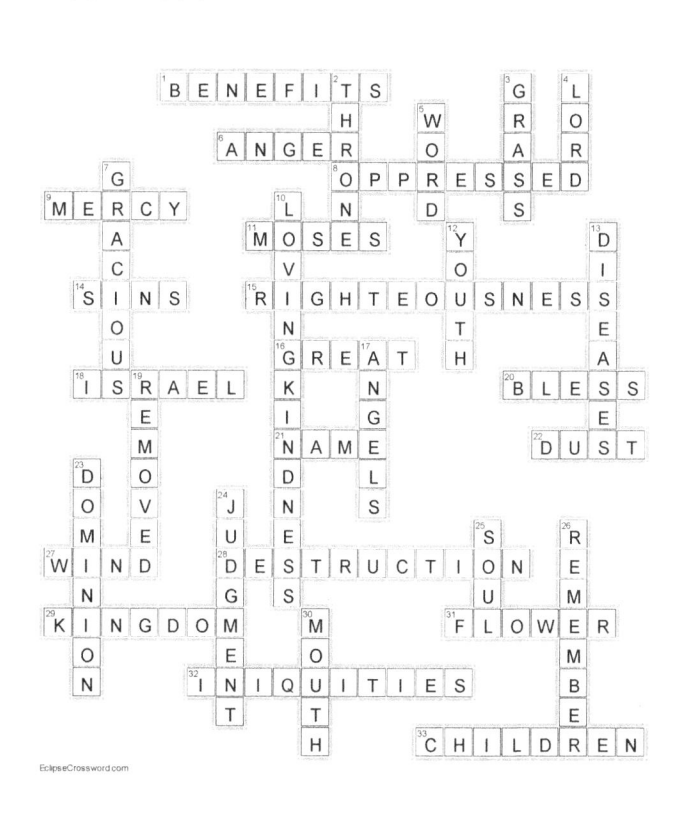

All Clues are taken directly from the 1611 edition of the King James Version (KJV).
Crossword Bible Studies: Top 40 Classic Songs in Psalms (KJV) © 2017 Christy Bower
These puzzles are reproducible if you purchased the book.
www.CrosswordBibleStudies.com

Psalm 107

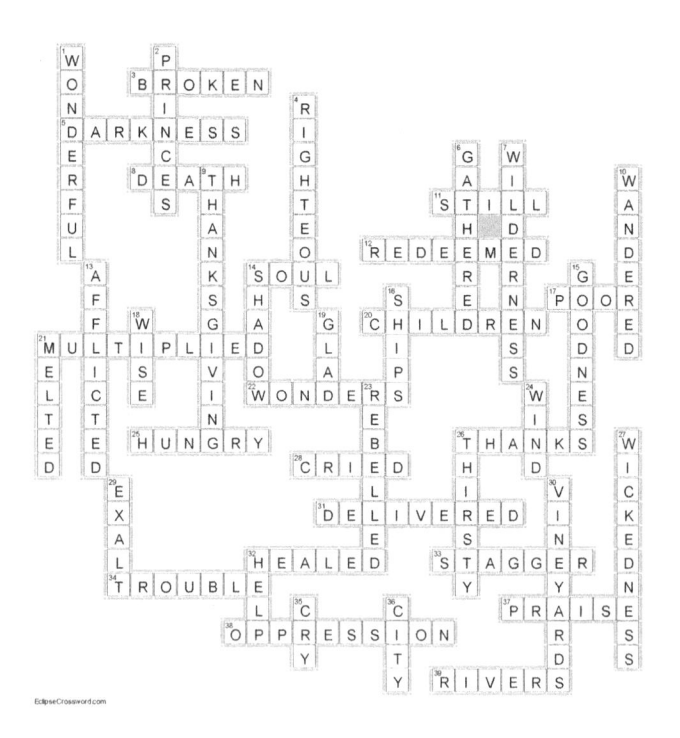

Psalm 115

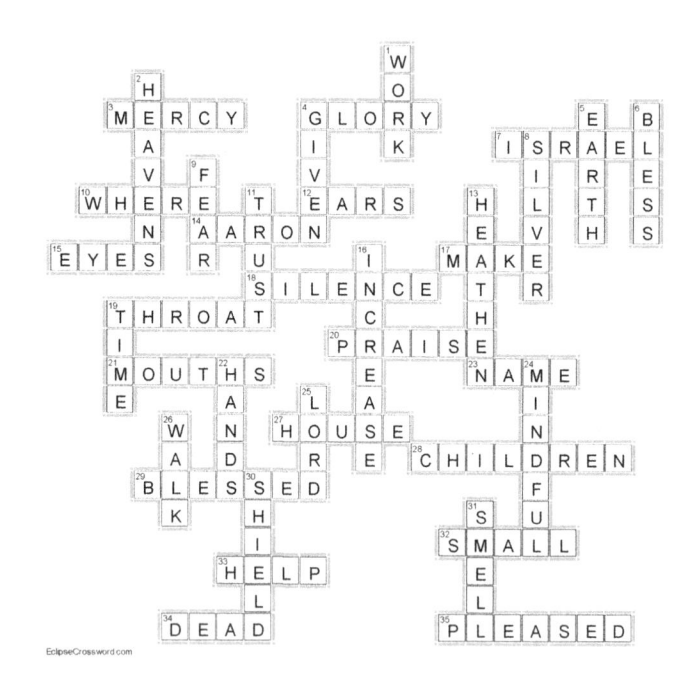

Psalm 112

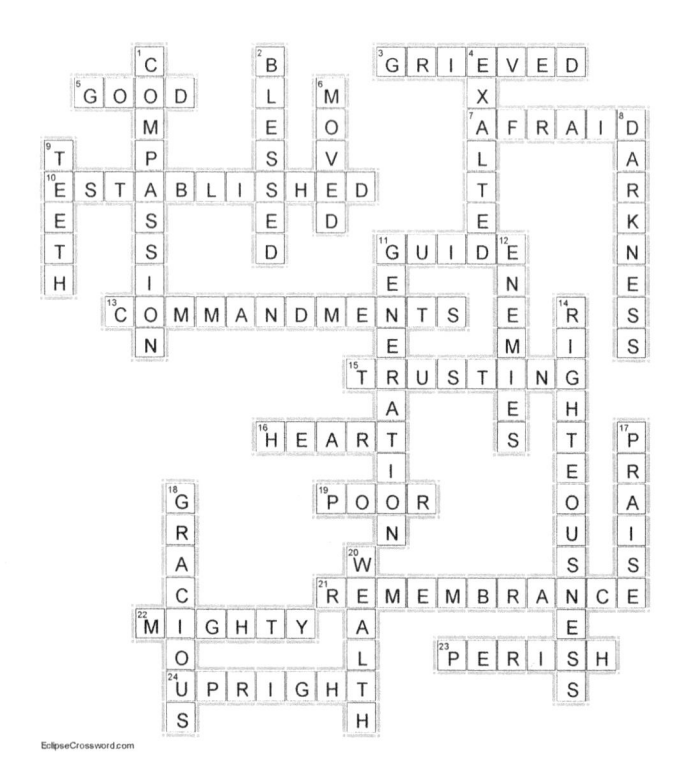

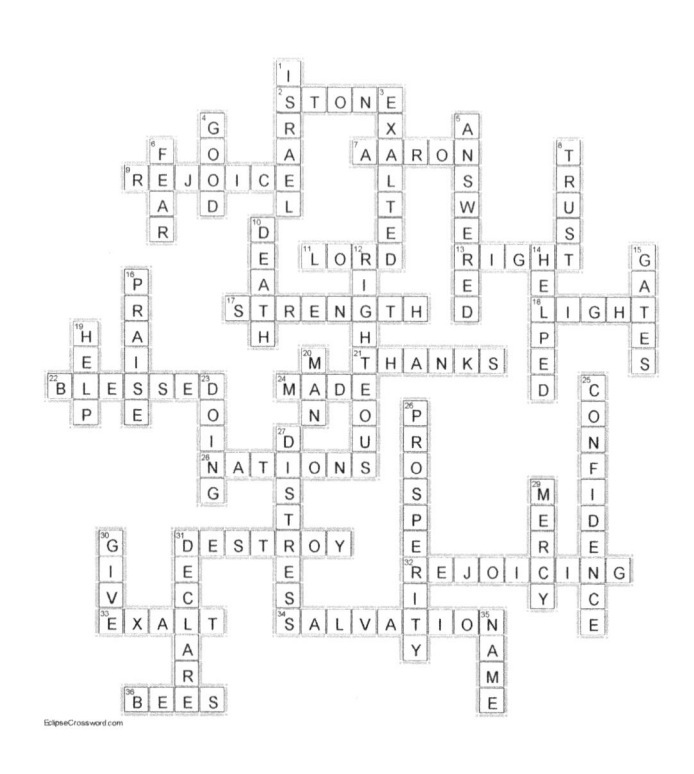

Psalm 118

All Clues are taken directly from the 1611 edition of the King James Version (KJV).
Crossword Bible Studies: Top 40 Classic Songs in Psalms (KJV) © 2017 Christy Bower
These puzzles are reproducible if you purchased the book.
www.CrosswordBibleStudies.com

Psalm 119

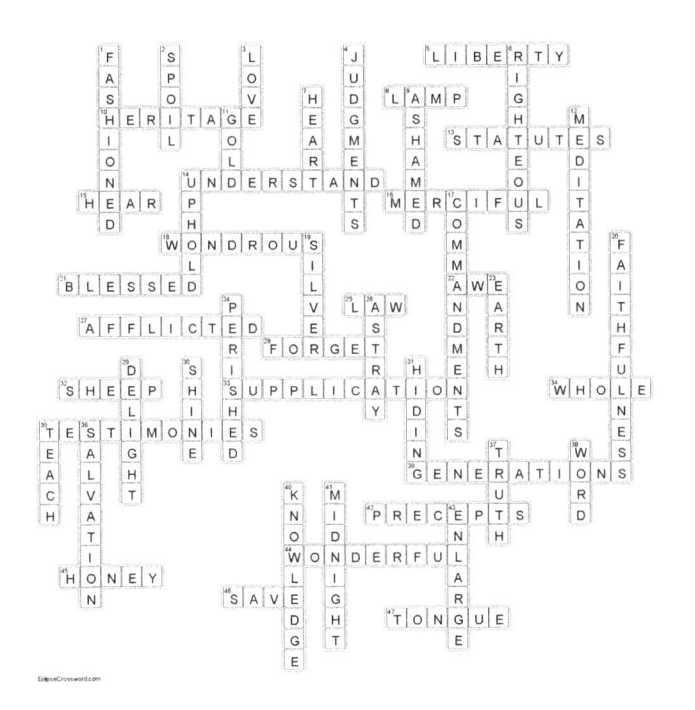

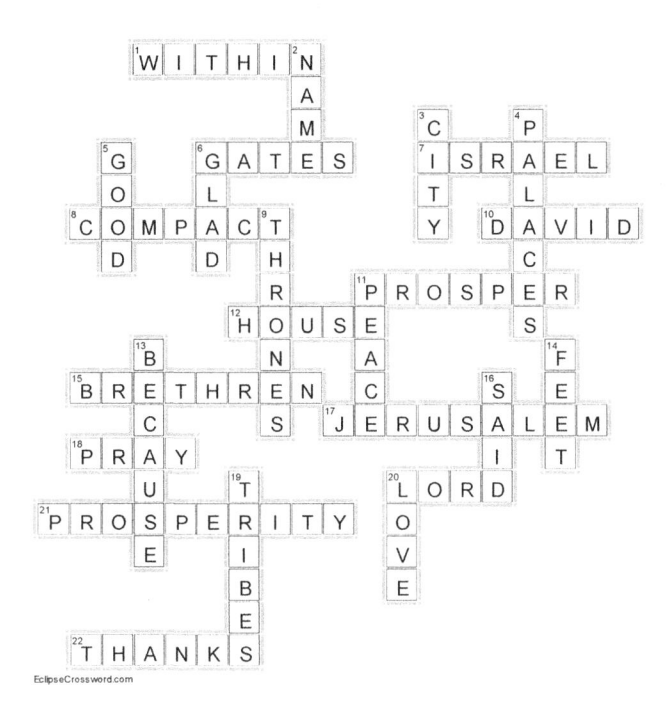

Psalm 122

Psalm 121

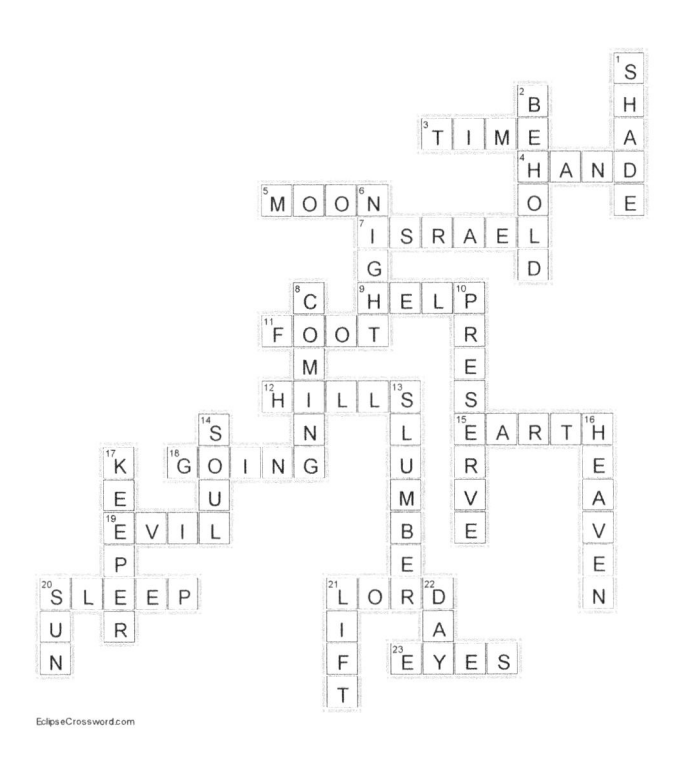

Psalm 136

All Clues are taken directly from the 1611 edition of the King James Version (KJV).
Crossword Bible Studies: Top 40 Classic Songs in Psalms (KJV) © 2017 Christy Bower
These puzzles are reproducible if you purchased the book.
www.CrosswordBibleStudies.com

Psalm 137

Psalm 139

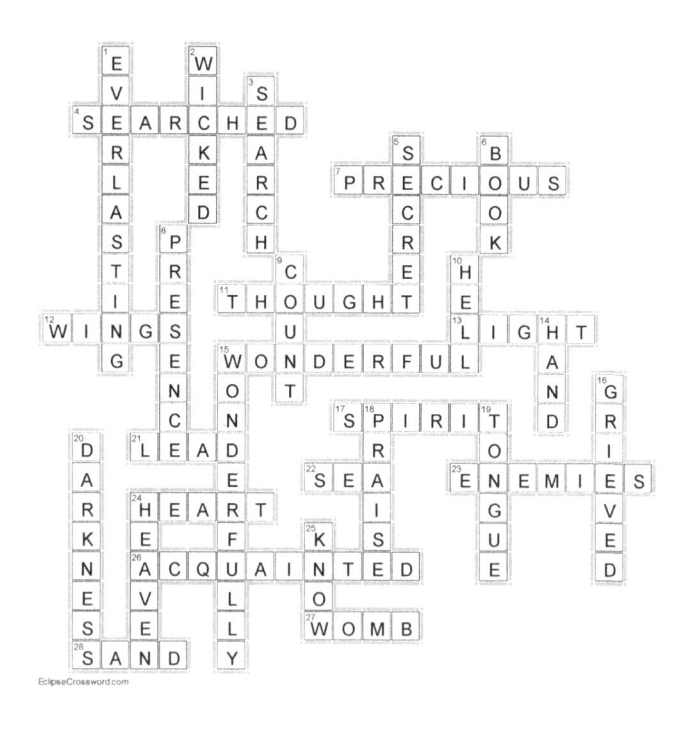

Psalm 138

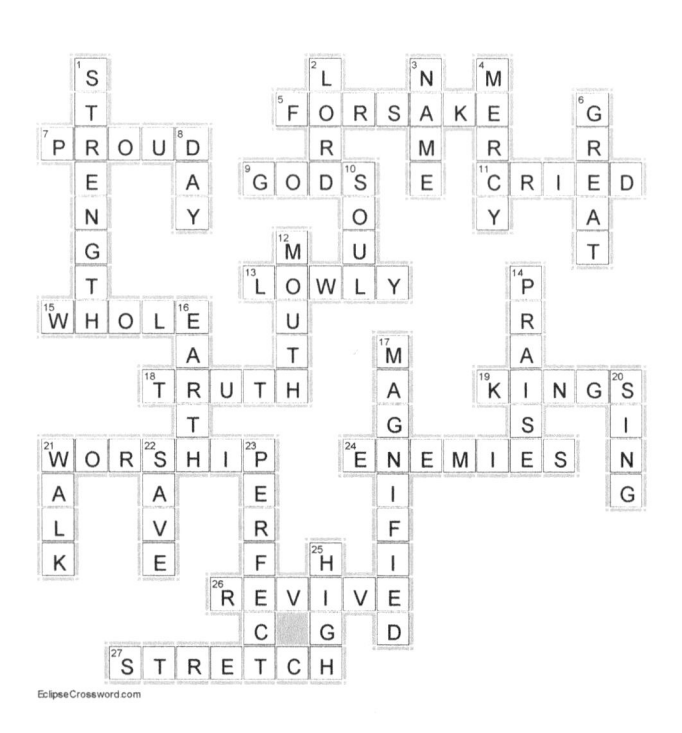

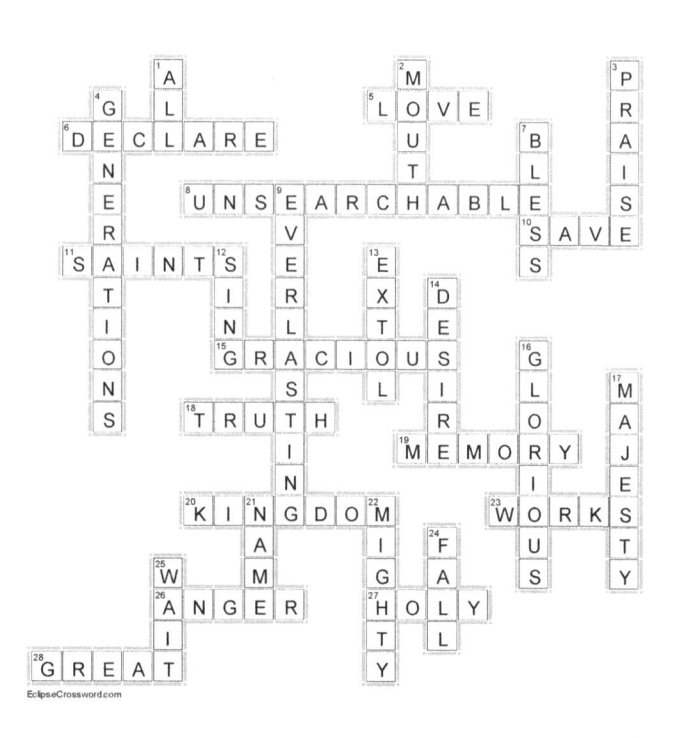

Psalm 145

All Clues are taken directly from the 1611 edition of the King James Version (KJV).
Crossword Bible Studies: Top 40 Classic Songs in Psalms (KJV) © 2017 Christy Bower
These puzzles are reproducible if you purchased the book.
www.CrosswordBibleStudies.com

Bonus Puzzle: Book of Psalms

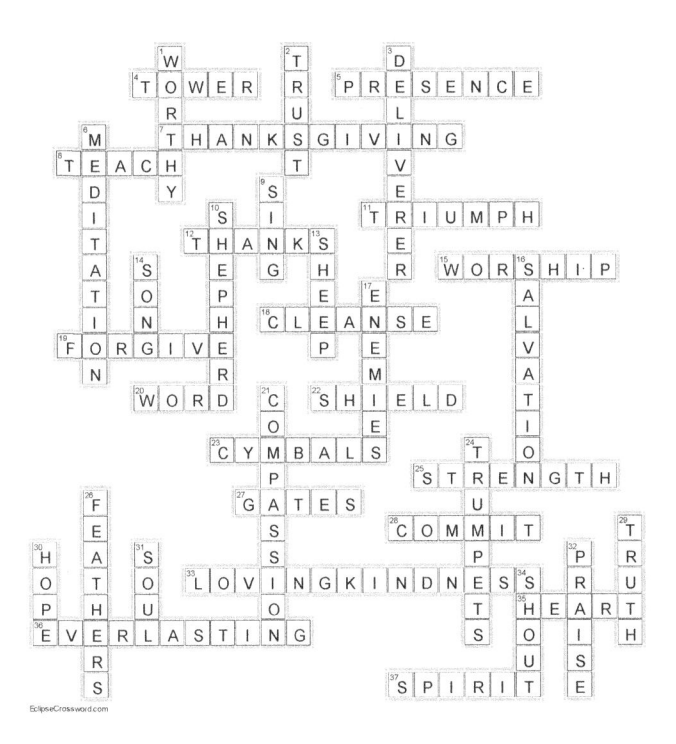

Made in the USA
Columbia, SC
27 February 2025